Why do share prices fall in May? When is the best time of year to buy a house? Is it true that mail order sales peak in November? And what is the mysterious 'M' factor – the common pattern that applies to so many different aspects of business and finance, even in other parts of the world?

These are just a few of the questions explored by Dr Thorneycroft in this fascinating study of seasonal behaviour across a wide range of social and economic activities. His analysis ranges from interest rates to holidays, form birth statistics to commodity prices, from violent crime to industrial output. All too often decision-makers in business, finance and government disregard seasonal influences. But Dr Thorneycroft shows that these influences can have a profound effect, not just in determining the shape of the future, but also in affecting the moods of the decision-makers themselves.

Policy makers, planners, forecasters and advisers in many walks of life will be grateful for Dr Thorneycroft's thought-provoking revelation. They provide the basis for a clearer understanding of the world we live in, and hence of better forecasts and better decisions.

The author

Dr Terry Thorneycroft trained as a chemical engineer and for many years worked for Shell Research Ltd. In 1964 he joined English China Clays, where he is now Corporate Planning Manager. He is a member of the Cornwall Industrial Development Association and of Information Technology South West.

SEASONAL PATTERNS IN BUSINESS AND EVERYDAY LIFE

Seasonal Patterns in Business and Everyday Life

Dr Terry Thorneycroft

Gower

Published by
Gower Publishing Company Limited,
Gower House,
Croft Road,
Aldershot,
Hants GU11 3HR,
England

British Library Cataloguing in Publication Data
Thorneycroft, Terry
  Seasonal patterns in business and everyday life.
  1. Seasonal variations (Economics)— Great Britain
  I. Title
  330.941'0858   HC256.6

  ISBN 0-566-02699-6

Set by Action Typesetting Ltd, Gloucester
Printed in Great Britain at the Alden Press, Oxford

Contents

List of Illustrations

Appendix I (b)

Preface

This book is, so far as I know, the first which comprehensively describes the seasonal patterns which exist in a wide variety of factors, of interest both to people in their everyday lives and to businessmen in particular.

My own interest in the subject was aroused when I came across pronounced seasonal patterns in measures of business confidence. To some extent, the subsequent work has been an attempt to identify the causes of those seasonal effects. In the process, I have broadened the study and, I hope, widened its appeal by extending it to include factors which we are all concerned about in our daily lives ... factors such as births and deaths; sickness and health; employment and unemployment; spending and saving.

I hope that the seasonal patterns which I portray will be of interest to everyone: I'm sure that you will find a few surprises! However, there is also a more serious objective to the work: understanding seasonal patterns is (or should be) an important factor in short-term business forecasting and planning. This is true of a company's own data (e.g. its sales pattern); it is also true of the world outside. Several times, in recent years, the business press has reported an upsurge in business confidence in the spring and, subsequently, a decline later in the year. Without an appreciation of seasonal behaviour patterns, it has been all too easy to misinterpret such reports as indicating significant shifts in the underlying trends in the economy.

This is not just a problem for individual businesses; I believe that a part of Britain's malaise can actually be traced to an unfortunate choice of timing for the annual Budget presentation by the Chancellor. By the time you reach the end of the book, you will no longer be surprised at how often an optimistic spring Budget has been superseded by corrective action, usually in July or in the autumn.

The analysis also clearly indicates some of the dangers which can arise from choosing November for the sale of major public assets such as shares in British Telecom.

Individual businessmen and investors alike will, I hope, find many examples of seasonal patterns which will be not only interesting but profitable to them as well.

Seasonal patterns are really just one special category of cycles (or repetitive rhythms) of various periods which have been detected in all kinds of data: economics, sunspots, agriculture, biology, sociology . . . indeed, almost anything which you can think of. The study of such cycles was pioneered by Edward R. Dewey who, until his death, was President of the Foundation for the Study of Cycles in the United States. His monumental work *Cycles—Selected Writings* is a remarkable compendium of several hundred cycles which have been reported. The periods of these cycles – that is, the time after which a similar pattern repeats itself – vary from 1 hour 4 minutes (the time between eruptions of the Old Faithful geyser) to 510 years (an alleged period of recurrence of civil wars). In between, he reports on cycles in an incredible range of subjects, as diverse as amorousness in women (2–4 weeks), the abundance of sooty terns (9.7 months), influenza (3 years), mice plagues (4 years) and church membership (9 years).

To me, the astonishing feature of Dewey's compilation is how *few* cycles are listed with a period of exactly one year; that is, events for which roughly the same pattern is reproduced each calendar year. The annual cycles of the weather, caused in turn by the regular and predictable revolution of the earth around the sun, and producing the regular growing cycles, might be expected to generate very many other 12-month cycles. In fact, the only other ones reported by Dewey were:

- earthquakes
- freight carried by the Canadian Pacific Railway
- pig iron (just what is not specified)
- plagues in Bombay

In fact, the last two are actually reported to recur with a period of 1 year and 4 days, rather than exactly one year.

Perhaps it's a case of the 12-month seasonal variations being taken for granted; I don't know. What I *have* found is that surprisingly little has been written about such seasonal patterns, despite the fact that they are perhaps the most obvious and consistently repetitive of all cycles.

One of the very few considerations of the economic significance of seasonal factors appeared in the August 1986 issue of the UK's *National Institute Economic Review*. In an article entitled 'Seasonal Patterns in the British Economy', the author, Andrew Britton, concluded that the analysis of seasonal variations in different economic series 'is a potentially rich, and largely unexploited, source of information about the way the economy works'.

I am sure that this is true. As you go through the book, you will get some idea of the very wide range of factors – economic and other – which exhibit a repetitive 12-month pattern.

Inevitably, this work has involved a huge task of data collection. I must particularly thank my wife, Jean, for the patience and care with which she has diligently extracted literally thousands of bits of information from various sources; also for her invaluable assistance in helping to edit and check the manuscript. Without her help and encouragement, producing this book would have been an impossible task.

The computer programming and the work of data entry were both carried out by the staff and students at the Cornwall ITeC; my thanks are due to them in very large measure, especially to Kevan Rudling and Kevin Gleeson. This Information Technology Centre is doing a splendid job in training hitherto unemployed youngsters to learn IT skills. It has been a great pleasure to have been able to associate them with the work.

I am also greatly indebted to my secretary, Diane Walker, both for typing the manuscript and for her ability to read my writing (no mean feat in itself!)

I am pleased to acknowledge the permission granted by my company, ECC International, to undertake this work; also the stimulating discussions with many colleagues.

Most of the data used for the study are readily available to the public, mainly in the excellent publications of the Central Statistical Office, namely the *Monthly Digest of Statistics, Economic Trends* and *Financial Statistics*. In other cases, I should like to acknowledge the sources listed in Appendix II. Although most of the examples are based on UK data, I have included several comparisons with data from the United States, Europe and the Pacific area.

Finally, I hope that you will be sufficiently interested in the subject to follow up your reading in a practical way. There are two ways in which you could do this. First, you may well wish to analyse some of your own data (for instance, your company's sales pattern or the price history of your favourite share); in the last section, I shall tell you how to go about this in a simple way. Secondly, you may like to offer a written contribution yourself on any aspect of the subject. If so, please write to me and – if there is sufficient interest – we may put together a sequel to this book, in the form of a compendium of the best contributions received.

Terry Thorneycroft
Duporth Bay,
St Austell,
Cornwall.

Part I
PROLOGUE

1 Introduction

If you were to open any book of official statistics, such as the *Monthly Digest of Statistics*, you would immediately notice that very many of the series of figures are presented in a form described as 'seasonally adjusted'. For many purposes for which the data are to be used, this is just what is needed.

For instance, two of the statistics which receive wide publicity each month are the inflation rate and the growth in earnings. The figures which we hear about in the news each month are the increases in inflation and earnings compared with the same time a year ago. Normally, we are not all that concerned about the details of the month-to-month variations which occur within the year. The closest we come to hearing about those variations is probably a mention of seasonal changes in the price of food.

We are all vaguely aware that there are seasonal variations in food prices, but probably can't quote any figures for the extent to which prices vary from one month to another. This is one of many factors we shall look at later. Similarly, we expect the level of retail sales to increase in December in anticipation of Christmas. Again, few people could say just how large this increase normally is for any particular type of retail outlet, and again this is something which will be portrayed in a subsequent chapter.

These patterns (not just around Christmas, but for the whole year) are lost in the 'seasonally adjusted' statistics. What the latter *do* provide – and what are for most purposes actually more useful – are measures of the underlying trends; e.g. whether retail sales are going up or down, or whether they are going up but at a slower rate. Businessmen in particular usually want to know, not that sales have increased by 25 per cent between November and December, but whether this represents a greater (or lesser) increase than would normally be expected at that time of the year. If so, it may confirm an increasing (or decreasing) underlying trend which can then be used to plan future production.

The job of working out these underlying trends is done for us by the statisticians. They have calculated the effects which are due to purely seasonal factors, such as Christmas, and corrected the data accordingly. So a tremendous amount of work is actually carried out all the time on seasonal factors; its objective, though, is not to *describe* the seasonal patterns but to *eliminate* them from the data.

Our task is just the opposite: we shall be removing the long-term trends and cycles, where they exist, so as to expose the seasonal patterns to full view.

Despite the large amount of work which has been carried out to remove seasonal effects, surprisingly little has been written about the nature of those effects themselves. So far as I know, this book represents the first attempt to set out the nature of the seasonal patterns for a wide range of factors.

There have, of course, been occasional mentions in technical journals of seasonality in specific factors. Of these, the one that has received most attention (and controversy) is interest rates. For that reason, I have included a separate chapter reviewing the historical evidence for and against significant seasonality in interest rates. Otherwise, literature on seasonal patterns is remarkably sparse, although I shall mention a few results which other people have published from time to time.

We shall be looking at a very wide range of factors, and I ought to say something about the way in which the results have been organized. The seasonal pattern charts have been subdivided into two sections: Part II of the book contains 'everyday life' factors and Part III the 'business' factors. However, I hope that everyone will find something of interest in both sections.

It is, in fact, impossible to make a clear distinction between the two sections. For instance, the seasonal patterns of retail sales of clothing are likely to be of interest to the general reader (as a customer of clothing shops) and also to many businessmen (whether they be retailers themselves or suppliers of clothing). Similarly, although I have included share prices in the 'business' section, I recognize that the buying and selling of shares is something of a hobby for a growing number of people in their everyday lives.

As the 'everyday life' section starts to overlap with the 'business' topics, you will be introduced to a phenomenon which I have called the M-factor. I have found that a wide range of business factors have a seasonal pattern shaped something like a letter 'M'. It might be business confidence, share prices, government stocks or one of several other factors: in each case, the annual pattern typically has two peaks (the top points of the 'M'), one around March/April and the other (usually a lower peak) around September/October. This monthly M-factor is to be found, not only in many different series of economic data, but also for many different countries and over several successive decades. The identification of this factor is probably the most important original contribution made in this book.

A perennial problem with official statistics, whether of the general interest or business variety, is that they are often published some time after the event to which they refer. This situation is improving all the time, but an additional problem remains. It is all too often the case that the figure first published is revised at a later date. For both of these reasons (not to mention the time taken to perform the analysis and write it up) it is impossible to use entirely up-to-date information. I have therefore used data mainly for 1975–84. In Part IV I have included a chapter based on 1985 and 1986 data. This not only brings some of the results further up to date, but it also serves to illustrate the extent to which the historical pattern is relevant to forecasting the future.

A technical appendix describes in more detail the mathematical methods and the computer program which have been used.

That appendix concludes with a brief note to help those who have been sufficiently interested in the results to want to pursue some analyses of their own. I have tried to include a wide range of subjects of general interest in the book, but I'm sure that each individual reader will find at least one of his favourite subjects missing. Also, each reader from the business world will have his or her own series of private data which are worthy of analysis.

There is no need to work through the book logically, chapter by chapter. If you really want to see whether you might make some money by knowing the seasonal patterns in exchange rates, there is no reason why you should not turn immediately to Chapter 24.

Occasionally, it has been necessary to introduce some technical points to clarify the main text. Such technical points have been inserted in separate boxes, aside from the main text, and can be treated as footnotes, to be read or not as you prefer.

The main purpose of the book is to present a compendium of facts, in the shape of the seasonal patterns inherent in many series of data. These facts themselves inevitably raise many questions (for instance, *why* are businessmen more confident at some times of the year than others?; *why* are interest rates lower and share prices higher in some months than in others?) I can't claim to know the answers to all – or indeed, to many – of the questions which you will start to ask yourself. I have given some opinions where it has seemed appropriate to do so. However, I am content to offer the facts (and perhaps a few clues) for you to consider for yourself. Meanwhile, I am sure that you will find the facts and figures themselves to be very useful, in understanding what is happening in the economy, in your business and in the world around you.

2 Twenty questions

for you to test your knowledge of seasonal factors

We all 'know' that oil prices are high in the winter and fall in the summer. Hence the 'third oil shock' in the winter of 1986 must have come as a shock in more senses than one: the collapse in prices occurred in the winter, and then prices recovered with the onset of summer. Should we really have been so surprised? I think not. The popular view of oil prices is just one of the myths which we shall question in the course of this book.

By way of introduction to a serious subject, let's start by taking a fairly lighthearted look at some of the other things which we think we know, instinctively, to be either true or false.

I've never really understood why people tend to forget that business can be fun, as well as being a very serious matter. Twenty-five years ago I worked in the research department of a large (and excellent) oil company. In the course of a technical report, I remember starting a sentence 'It was amusing to note that . . .'. Now, I have absolutely no idea today just what it was that caused this amusement; what I *do* still remember clearly is the reprimand which followed! In those days, amusement had no place in business.

Today's businessmen are much more aware of the fact that fun can be a positive aid to understanding. Management and business games have been developed to a fine art, both as a method of learning new techniques and as a method of testing the effects of alternative business strategies; these games are not only very useful learning tools, but they are also fun.

So, on pages 7 and 8 are twenty questions, on subjects which are discussed in more detail in the chapters which follow. All you have to do is to tick one of the boxes after each question, depending on whether you believe each statement to be True or False. The answers are given in the pages which follow.

The seasonal patterns given in the book are calculated after having removed the effects of any long-term trends or cycles in the data. For instance, if house prices were to rise steadily all the time, then the price at the end of the year would naturally be higher than the price at the beginning of the year. What we are interested in − and what is shown in the book − are the monthly variations, up and down, *from the trend line*. The way in which we calculate these deviations is described in Chapter 3. The point to remember now, in answering the quiz, is that the questions refer to these monthly deviations from any longer-term trends which are present.

There is just one additional question which you may like to think about now. In this case, the answer is not a choice between True and False, but is a specific month of the year. The question is:

> In which month should a British Conservative government choose to have a General Election, in order to maximize its chances of being re-elected for a further term of office?

The answer to this question is hidden away in one of the later chapters. You may find it interesting to see whether any of the seasonal patterns which you encounter en route give any clues to the answer.

Meanwhile good luck with the quiz! I hope that it gives you the flavour of what is to follow later in the book.

TWENTY QUESTIONS

		TRUE	FALSE
1	On average, June is the dryest month in the year.	☐	☐
2	House prices are relatively low in February and highest in May.	☐	☐
3	The birth rate is high in September, nine months after the Christmas party season.	☐	☐
4	The most popular month for going to the cinema is August.	☐	☐
5	The peak month for weddings is either March or April, depending when Easter falls.	☐	☐
6	Deaths due to respiratory diseases (e.g. bronchitis) are highest in the winter, whereas you are just as likely to die from heart disease at any time of the year.	☐	☐

		TRUE	FALSE
7	The peak month for sickness is January.	☐	☐
8	After August, the next month most popular for UK residents travelling abroad is September.	☐	☐
9	Crimes of violence against other people reach a peak in late summer.	☐	☐
10	Jewellery shops do more than twice as much business in December as in any other month of the year.	☐	☐
11	Mail order sales reach a peak, not in December but in November.	☐	☐
12	Industrial output is at a particularly low ebb in December and January, because of the extended Christmas holidays.	☐	☐
13	The quantity of money in circulation with the public is at its highest in December.	☐	☐
14	Similarly, money in building society accounts is run down in December, to help finance Christmas shopping.	☐	☐
15	On the other hand, premium bond sales increase in December, suggesting that many are given as Christmas presents.	☐	☐
16	Men, more than women, tend to wait for the January and summer sales before buying their clothes.	☐	☐
17	A stock market adage is 'sell in May and go away'; this reflects the fact that share prices tend to reach a peak in May.	☐	☐
18	The corollary of this is that interest rates are at their lowest in May.	☐	☐
19	The London stock market tends to follow (or reflect) seasonal changes in the Wall Street stock market.	☐	☐
20	It is best to buy pesetas for your Spanish holiday well ahead of the actual holiday period, since the high demand for pesetas in the summer results in a poorer rate of exchange.	☐	☐

ANSWERS

1 FALSE. Rainfall patterns vary tremendously from one year to another, but on average March and April have slightly lower rainfall than June. (On wet days in June, the rainfall tends to be heavier than in the spring). The wettest month is November.

2 TRUE. The difference between February and May is not all that large – about 2 per cent; however, the pattern is a very distinct one. From May onwards, the purely seasonal component of prices tends to drift downwards until the following February.

3 TRUE.

4 TRUE, and by a very wide margin. It may seem surprising that cinema-going is highest in the summer. It is presumably associated with the school holidays; also, going to the cinema is a popular way of escaping the rain on summer holidays. Cinema attendances in August are half as much again as in the lowest month (June).

5 FALSE. In fact, the whole of the spring period (March to May) has just about the annual average rate of weddings. The numbers start rising quickly from June onwards, reaching a substantial peak in August and September.

6 FALSE. Deaths from heart disease follow a strong seasonal pattern very similar to that for respiratory diseases – which means that they are high in the winter and low in the summer. Cancer deaths, on the other hand, *are* distributed fairly evenly throughout the year.

7 FALSE. It is often imagined that people are at their lowest ebb in winter. December and January are actually not bad months for health. The worst months are February and March. The precise peak varies from year to year, but on average the worst month for sickness is actually March.

8 TRUE. You may have expected trips abroad to be higher in July than in September; that *is* the case for foreign visitors coming to the UK; also for British residents travelling to the USA. However, travel to Europe and other areas (holidays plus business travel) is very high in September.

9 TRUE. The July–September quarter is a relatively quiet time for most of the common offences – theft, burglary, robbery, criminal damage. On the other hand, man's aggressive instincts – as measured by attacks on other people (both 'violence against the person' and sexual offences) – do rise to a peak towards the end of the summer.

10   TRUE. Of all of the series illustrated in this book, the seasonal pattern of jewellery sales is the most pronounced. December sales are actually about two-and-a-half times those in any other month except November.

11   TRUE. Purchases by mail order tend to be made rather further ahead of Christmas than is the case with conventional retail outlets. This is not surprising; what is perhaps unexpected is that mail order sales are also high in January; don't forget that mail order companies, just as much as other retail outlets, can have their January sales.

12   FALSE. Total industrial output in both December and January is only fractionally below the yearly average, although some 5 per cent below the March and November peaks. The really low period for output is associated with the holiday months of July and August.

13   TRUE. The amount of money in circulation increases in December and then immediately declines sharply in January.

14   FALSE. There is an increase in withdrawals in November, but December is actually the best month in the year for building society accounts; this is largely due to the crediting of year-end interest payments.

15   FALSE. December actually has the *lowest* monthly sales of premium bonds, 20 per cent below the annual average.

16   TRUE. The peak month for sales of both men's wear and women's wear is December. However, in the 'sale' months of January and July the sales of men's wear is relatively higher than women's wear.

17   TRUE. Share prices on average certainly tend to be higher at the end of April than at the end of May, by perhaps 4 per cent. Averaged over the whole month, April and May are not very different, which suggests that you should sell early on in May. Remember that this conclusion is based on the seasonal factor alone, after eliminating any trend. If you think that share prices are in (or are about to start) a downward trend, then the safer bet would seem to be to sell in April, rather than May.

18   FALSE. Whilst the ups and downs of interest rates do, in general, mirror seasonal share price movements, the turning point in the spring comes rather earlier. Interest rates are at their lowest (i.e. bond prices are highest) in March and April. Incidentally, the comments above about share prices apply to the average of a wide variety of shares; the prices of shares of financial companies tend to peak in March/April, more in line with the interest rate pattern.

19 FALSE. As far as the shorter-term seasonal pattern is concerned, there is absolutely no similarity at all. In fact, in recent years it would be stretching the imagination to find any real similarities in the longer-term movements either.

20 FALSE. Not only is it false, but it is the worst thing you could do. You are likely to get slightly *more* pesetas to the pound from June to August; what is more, by converting your money earlier, you would have lost the interest which you would otherwise have been earning. The largest demand for pesetas is around October; this must have something to do with the arrangements which are being made by tour operators in advance of the booking season for the following year.

3 Calculating the seasonal patterns

At this stage, before we launch into the actual results, I ought to say a little bit about the techniques used for calculating seasonal effects; also about the ways in which the results are going to be presented. Those of you who are familiar with the subject may like to move straight on to Part II.

For those who are not so familiar, I will go through the principles in outline; more details are given in Appendix I. Don't worry if you find the description in this chapter a bit too technical. It's not essential to work your way through it in order to enjoy the results of the analyses. For those who *do* study this chapter, I hope that the subsequent results will mean just a little more than they might otherwise have done.

There is no one 'correct' method of calculating seasonal factors. The method which I shall describe is actually one of the simplest; it is also, in my experience, just as good as any other method for our descriptive purposes. However, I ought to start by mentioning some other types of analysis which are useful under particular circumstances.

Methods for detecting significant seasonality

One class of techniques is useful for deciding whether a significant seasonal pattern exists or not, without actually establishing what that seasonal pattern looks like. Within this category are two basic methods which calculate, respectively, what are called the 'auto-correlation function' and 'spectral analysis' of a time series. Since they do not produce a picture of the seasonal pattern (if one exists), they are not relevant to our purpose.

Regression methods

The statistical technique of regression analysis can be adapted to calculate seasonal factors. It is a method which has its adherents; however, more has been written on the theory than on its practical application. I shall refer to it further in Appendix I.

Moving average methods

The method most widely used in practice by official statisticians goes under the rather forbidding title of 'The X-11 variant of the Census Method II Seasonal Adjustment Program' produced by the US Bureau of the Census. It is more commonly abbreviated to the 'X-11' method.

The Bureau has researched seasonal analysis for many years, and 'X-11' incorporates the most up-to-date developments of its work. It first appeared in 1965, and it is indicative of its power and flexibility that no subsequent variants have been issued. No study of seasonal analysis would be complete without due reference to this work. In Appendix I, as well as describing its main features, I shall also use it as a benchmark against which to compare my own approach. (To anticipate the outcome, the two methods give almost identical results).

The key to its value lies in the word 'adjustment' in the full title. It is particularly useful if you want to *adjust* new data, as they become available, so as to *eliminate* the seasonal effects. It is an excellent method for eliminating the seasonal effects in this way, so as to highlight the underlying long-term trends. It is also the method to be preferred if you want to *predict* the seasonal pattern over the next few months.

Its value for these purposes arises from the fact that it gives more weight to more recent data. (It also contains several other refinements.) As I said in the Introduction, our task is to *describe* seasonal patterns rather than to *eliminate* or *predict* them. For our purposes, it is actually more relevant to use a simpler technique, which calculates the *average* seasonal pattern over a period of about ten years. This relatively simple 'moving average' calculation is what I shall now outline.

The components of a time series

Les us start by taking a practical example. Suppose that we have a monthly sales graph that looks like this:

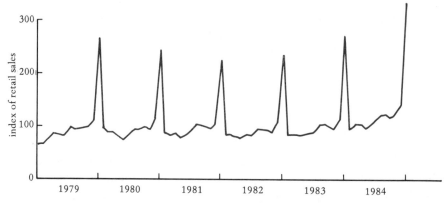

The first thing you are likely to say, on seeing this graph, is that it is probably fictitious. In fact, it isn't. It is the actual monthly pattern of sales by jewellers from 1979 to 1984.

The most obvious feature of the graph is the very sharp peak each December. Christmas affects many of the series of data which we shall be looking at in Part II, but none more so than jewellery sales. As we saw in the quiz, December sales are more than *twice* those for any other month of the year. Although several series show a December peak, and several other series show sharp seasonal peaks at other times of the year, it is unusual to find such a pronounced seasonal pattern as this one. In some of the examples we shall look at in Parts II and III, the maximum seasonal effect is no more than 1 or 2 per cent.

If we look more closely at this sales chart, we can detect some of the other features which characterize most series of historical data. Since 1982, there has been an upward *trend* in sales. Very many series have quite pronounced trends which dominate all else. For instance, over most periods of time, the levels of house prices and of average earnings show upward trends, due to inflation, which dominate and obscure the relatively small seasonal effects; the latter can only be worked out by careful analysis.

Coming back to jewellery sales, no such upward trend existed in the period 1979–82. In fact, if we look at the complete graph (certainly at the December peaks) we might well conclude that there is some kind of *cycle* in the data, i.e. good years interspersed by not-so-good years. Almost all factors which are of interest in economics and business life exhibit some such cycle to a greater or lesser extent. In recent years, the typical business cycle has had a period of 4 or 5 years, popularly described as the 'stop–go' cycle. In other words, there have been peaks in economic activity every 4 years or so, with lower activity or a genuinely recessionary period in between. The years 1980 to 1982 will be remembered as being the time of a particularly long-drawn-out recession, before activity picked up again in 1983. Such cycles affect all aspects of economic life, not excluding the peak rate of jewellery sales around Christmas time, as we can see in the chart.

Seasonal effects, trends and cycles may go a long way towards accounting for much of the month-to-month variation in jewellery sales, but cannot account for every little change in the graph. The residual, unexplained variations are called *random* (or *irregular*) effects.

So, to summarize, a long series of monthly data is likely to contain, to a greater or lesser extent:

- a long-term trend
- one or more cycles
- seasonal effects
- random variations

There is one other possibility (namely a sudden step-change) which I shall come back to later, but meanwhile we shall stay with this traditional way of subdividing a time series into its component parts.

In most economic analyses, it is actually the trends and the cycles which are of greatest interest. In our case, we need first to *eliminate* the contributions made to the month-to-month variations by those trends and cycles, in order to highlight the seasonal patterns. The means of doing this is to calculate what are called 12-month moving averages.

Moving averages

In order to describe this process, I shall still use the kind of data illustrated by jewellery sales, but in a highly simplified form, as shown in the following chart.

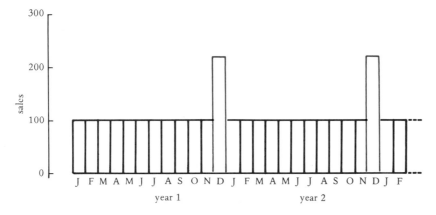

In this hypothetical example, sales are at a uniform level of 100 units from January to November and 220 units in December. This means that the total for the year is 1,320 units and the monthly average is 110 units.

Suppose, for the moment, that there is no trend or cycle; in other words, that the pattern illustrated above is repeated exactly each year. Then it does not matter where we choose to start a 12-month period; the annual total will be 1,320 (and the monthly average 110), whether we choose a 12-month period starting in January, February, March, or any other month. Whatever period of 12 months we choose will contain 11 months of 'normal' sales and one December.

This is an example of what is meant by a '12-month moving average' of a set of data: it is a sequence of average values for each 12-month period, starting with the first 12 months of the series of data and moving forward one month at a time. Each time we take a step forward, we drop off the data for the earliest month and add on the next month in the time series; in that way, each value we calculate is the average of 12 consecutive months.

Calculating the seasonal effect

Since the 12-month moving average includes one data point for each month of the year, it automatically averages out any seasonal effects which might be present. In fact, it gives a picture of the underlying long-term level of annual sales and of any trends and cycles that exist. The seasonal effect itself is then calculated, for each month, by *subtracting* the 12-month moving average from the *actual* level for that month. In our example, this calculation would produce the following result:

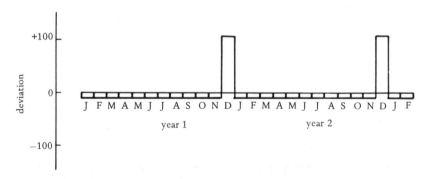

The seasonal factor (i.e. the deviation from the 12-month moving average) is −10 units for each month from January to November inclusive and +110 units for December.

In real life, the deviations will not be as repetitive as in this example.

Although December may (as in the case of jewellery sales) always be very high, the precise magnitude of this seasonal peak will vary from year to year. The final step, then, is to average − for each month − each year's estimate of the seasonal deviation for that month. So, for our hypothetical example, the final result would be:

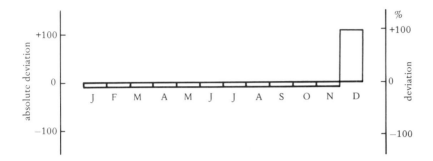

Two slightly different scales are illustrated for the magnitude of the seasonal effects. On the left of the diagram, the seasonal deviations are shown in terms of their absolute values (e.g. −10 units for January, +110 units for December); on the right of the diagram is an alternative presentation, where the scale shows the monthly seasonal deviations as *percentages* of the annual average (which in this case is 110 units). In most instances in the book, I shall show the magnitude of the seasonal pattern in this latter way, as a percentage deviation from the average level.

In a real-life case, that annual average itself will be changing, due to the effects of trends and cycles. The method of calculating the seasonal pattern in such cases is exactly the same as above, except that for each month we have to subtract the actual value for that month from the *particular* 12-month moving average centred on that month. This leads to one minor refinement. If we average the results for each month from January to December for a particular year, then the midpoint of the year corresponds to neither June nor July but halfway between the two. What we then do is to calculate also the 12-month moving average for the period from February to the following January; the midpoint of *this* 12-month period is halfway between July and August. By averaging these *two* 12-month moving averages, we get a good estimate of the 12-month moving average centred on July. The seasonal factor for July is then calculated by subtracting this moving average from the actual value for July.

This probably all sounds very complicated, but it isn't really. The process is more clearly illustrated by a simple example (as shown in the table). In this example, there is a steady upward trend in the original data, and no separate seasonal effect. Hence we can anticipate that the calculated seasonal factors will be zero.

Year	Month	Monthly data	Average Jan–Dec	Average Feb–Jan	Moving average for Jul	Seasonal factor for Jul
1	Jan	100				
	Feb	110				
	Mar	120				
	Apr	130				
	May	140				
	Jun	150	} 155			
	Jul	160		} 165	} 160	0
	Aug	170				
	Sep	180				
	Oct	190				
	Nov	200				
	Dec	210				
2	Jan	220				

You will see that, in fact, 13 months' data are needed in order to calculate the moving average for each month. The technical term for this is a 'centred 12-month moving average' and this is what I shall really mean in future when I refer to '12-month moving averages' or just 'moving averages'.

In the above example, the data showed a steady upward trend of 10 units per month, with no specifically seasonal effect. In such a situation, the 12-month moving average for any particular month will be the same as the original value for that month, giving a seasonal effect of zero. This can be seen in the example shown in the table. If the actual July figure had *differed* from its 12-month moving average, that difference would then have been a measure of the seasonal effect *plus* the random, unpredictable component of that month's figure. By definition, the random component is equally likely to be positive or negative. Therefore, if we average the July deviations over several years, these positive and negative random effects will tend to cancel each other out, leaving an average deviation which will be very largely a measure of the seasonal effect alone. (In the process, we can also test whether the resulting seasonal effect is statistically significant, but we won't go into that at this point). That, then, is a simplified description of how we go about calculating the seasonal patterns.

The method which I have described, of calculating the deviations from the moving averages, eliminates the effects of long-term trends (as shown above) and largely eliminates the effects of any business cycle or other long-term cycle in the data. Unlike trends, cycles do actually cause some technical problems in calculating a true measure of the seasonal effect, as discussed in Appendix I.

Prior corrections to the data

Most sets of data contain one or more 'rogue' values, or 'outliers' as they are usually termed − in other words, values which seem to be rather out of line with the rest of the data. For instance, in the series of values for jewellery sales, we would rightly have been very suspicious if the data indicated that sales had doubled for just one month in the middle of one summer.

Sometimes, an apparent outlier is simply due to an error in the published statistics. This, fortunately, happens only rarely. However, even the most reputable organizations are bound to make occasional mistakes; in the chapter on exchange rates, I refer to one such error in Bank of England statistics.

Using the X-11 method, it is actually possible to choose to ignore any values which lie outside pre-assigned levels of probability. I have to say that I am not generally in favour of doing this; I prefer to treat all data as genuine unless there is a very good, specific reason for not doing so.

One such good reason is the occurrence of a strike. For instance, in one year a strike of customs officials distorted the monthly pattern of customs and excise duties. In such cases, I *have* first estimated what the actual results would have looked like without a strike. (A strike can also occur − indeed *has* occurred − amongst the people responsible for compiling the statistics; again, in such cases, I have estimated what the data would have been.

Dealing with 'shocks' or step-changes in the data

We have just considered the case of 'outliers' − occasions where, just for one month (or a few adjacent months), the values appear to be abnormal; the data series then reverts to its earlier pattern.

There is another class of events which we need to consider. In some cases, there is a sudden change in a series of data which is *not* just a temporary phenomenon. We occasionally encounter 'shocks' to a series of data, which move the whole series up (or down) to a completely new level. At the time of writing, we have just experienced such step-changes (downwards) in the prices of both tin and oil. In principle, these events could have occurred at any time of the year. Such events create real problems for seasonal analysis: if we are looking at the seasonal prices of tin or oil, do we include in our calculations the months in which these 'shocks' occur? Or do we regard them as unique, isolated events which − because they could have happened at any time of the year – should be ignored (because otherwise they would distort whatever longer-term seasonal effects exist)?

This is one of the most difficult problems of seasonal analysis, and the possibility is usually ignored. In Appendix I, I shall describe how such shocks generate a particular kind of seasonal pattern.

As with outliers, I prefer *not* to try to adjust the data for such events. Although such events *may* appear to occur out of the blue at any time, and at any month in the year, I believe that they are not really quite so random.

For instance, a sudden drop in the price of a commodity may *appear* to be caused by quite extraneous events, but in practice I have found that such a situation is most likely to come to a head when the commodity (or whatever it is that we are studying) is in a period of seasonal weakness anyway; and that the price collapse is just an extreme manifestation of the seasonal pattern. We shall see this situation dramatically illustrated when we come to look at the month-to-month variations in interest rates at the times of the two OPEC oil 'shocks'; furthermore, the subsequent oil price collapse in January/March 1986 coincided precisely with the months when 'spot' oil prices tend to be weak anyway. (You may have expected an oil price collapse in mid-summer rather than towards the end of winter; this is just one of the many surprises in the results which will be illustrated.)

Indeed, it is a particular conclusion of this work that seasonal effects are *most* pronounced at times of rapid underlying change. Contrary to what I imagine would be popular belief, sharp changes in factors such as price levels do *not* swamp seasonal effects.

So, in general, I have not tried to correct or compensate for such events. The one exception to this rule is when an out-of-line event occurred right at the beginning of the 10-year period, i.e. in 1975 or 1976. In such cases, I *have* chosen to omit the first year(s) from the analysis. In that way, the patterns which are shown are more likely to be equally relevant today.

Presentation of the results

In almost all cases, the results are given as monthly seasonal factors. Unfortunately, in just a few cases it was only possible to obtain quarterly data. The method used to analyse quarterly data is no different in principle from that for monthly data.

Just before we move on to look at the actual results, I ought to explain the two common forms of representation:

Quantities. Where the data refer to a physical quantity (e.g. a level of output), the seasonal pattern is shown in the form of a bar chart, e.g.

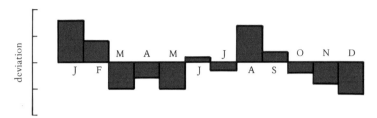

Levels. With many sets of data, the value being measured is an interest rate or the value of an index (e.g. of prices or of shares). In such cases, the monthly seasonal factors are shown as points which are joined together by straight lines:

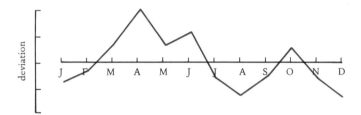

This distinction has occasionally been waived in the interests of clarity, but in general it is the convention which has been adopted for the descriptive sections of the book, which follow.

In just a few cases, I have also deviated from the use of the moving-average method of calculation; such cases are clearly indicated in the text.

Now that you have been introduced to the method, I hope that you feel suitably prepared to look at the results of using the method to analyse real-life time series.

Part II
EVERYDAY LIFE

4 Weather

When we think of seasonal changes it's usually the weather that we have in mind, and things which are directly affected by the weather. So this is a good place to start, although by the time you reach the end of the book you will have been introduced to seasonality in a very wide range of other things as well.

Apart from the obvious seasonal changes, the most pronounced feature of the British weather is its variability, which is why people spend so much time talking about it. Visitors to this country (other than Americans) are amazed at the sophistication and complexity of our TV weather forecasts. The Americans, on the other hand, may not be any *better* than the English at this pastime, but they certainly do *more* of it! You may know that they have one television channel devoted entirely to continuous, all-day weather forecasting. I can remember, one day in a hotel in Boston, being astonished by the ingenuity of each separate television channel in coming up with its own original way of presenting the weather forecast. Even more amazing was the fact that the forecasts themselves were so different from each other!

The differences which we are looking at in this book are those which occur from month to month, averaged over a period of many years. The charts in Figure 4.1 are all for England and Wales and they comprise:

Temperature: mean daily air temperature at sea level.
Sunshine: mean daily sunshine.
Rainfall: average total rainfall for each month.

The last of these, being a monthly total rather than a daily average, will tend to understate February *daily* rainfall by about 10 per cent.

Of the three weather factors which are illustrated, rainfall has by far the

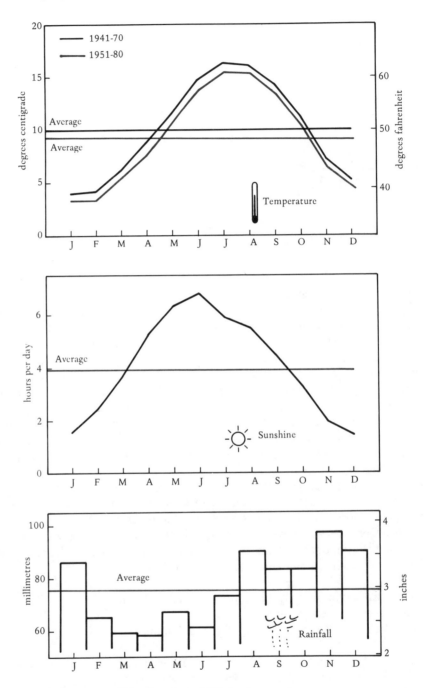

Fig. 4.1   Weather (England and Wales)

greatest year-to-year variation for any one month. On average, April is one of the dryest months in the year with a long-term mean rainfall of 58 millimetres (2.285 inches). In two recent years, 1983 and 1984, April rainfall was respectively 108 mm (4¼ inches) and 11 mm (less than half an inch). The highest recorded monthly rainfall in the UK was 1,436 mm (56½ inches) at Llyn Llydau, Snowdon, during October 1909.

Two sets of average temperature figures are given in Figure 4.1, namely for 1941–70 and 1951–80. These periods overlap considerably, and it is therefore surprising to find as much as 0.6°C (1°F) difference between the two graphs. This means that the difference in average temperature between the warm 1940s and the cooler 1970s was as much as 3°F. The general shape of the seasonal pattern has not changed.

In the next chapter, we shall be looking at births, marriages and deaths. The weather patterns strongly influence all three of these, none more so than the death rate. The number of deaths which occur each month is almost a mirror image of the monthly temperature pattern. One difference to look out for is July, which doesn't quite follow this relationship: too much heat can be a problem as well as too much cold.

5 Births, marriages and deaths

Whereas the average weather pattern is well known, there are likely to be some surprises in what are called 'vital statistics'.

I've used two different methods for analysing the seasonal patterns shown in this chapter. For births, marriages, divorces and road fatalities, I have used the preferred method of looking at deviations from 12-month moving averages. This is the method which was described in Chapter 3. Most death statistics, on the other hand, are based on a detailed analysis of one particular year, as I shall explain below. Meanwhile, we shall start by looking at birth rates.

Births

The results for births are given in Figure 5.1a. The year is subdivided fairly clearly into two parts:

March–September: relatively high birth rates
October–January: relatively low birth rates

The 'odd man out' seems to be August. The difference between the September peak and the December low is about 10 per cent.

If we assume a constant gestation period of 9 months (the average gestation period of 267 days is actually about 8¾ months), we can have a look at the pattern of successful conceptions. This may offer an explanation for the apparent August anomaly in the birth rate.

With the exception of December, conception rates follow a fairly smooth

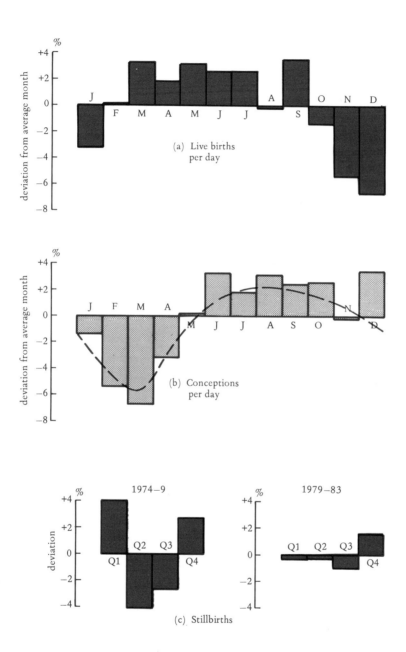

(a) Live births
      per day

(b) Conceptions
      per day

1974–9

1979–83

(c) Stillbirths

Fig. 5.1   Births

pattern over the year, as shown by the dotted curve in Figure 5.1b. Activity is low in the winter and early spring and then rises in the summer. I am tempted to think that the December anomaly may be connected in some way with the Christmas festivities. This pattern also indicates that it is not August which has an unusually *low* birth rate, it is more a matter of the September figure being *high*.

There is a comment on this Christmas effect in Dewey's compendium, *Cycles — Selected Writings*, referred to in the Preface. Dewey refers to a study by a Mr Curtis Jackson, Controller of the Methodist Hospital of Southern California, who detected a 29½-day cycle in births in the period 1939–1944. Significantly more children were born in his hospital during the waxing phase (new moon to full moon) than in the waning phase (full moon to new moon). In just a few cases, this rhythm was broken; to quote:

> Some of the distortions would seem to have possible explanations. For example, the fourth waning phase from the right (i.e. from the end of the year) in the years 1940, 1942, 1943 and 1944 came just about nine months after the Christmas–New Year parties of 1939, 1941, 1942 and 1943 respectively. (In 1938 and 1941 the period of Christmas and New Year festivities coincided with the waxing phase of the moon, and the period nine months later shows no distortion.)

We are not told whether the Methodist Controller was shocked by the discovery of this Christmas party effect. Probably not; he seems to have had a sense of humour, as he describes his sample as comprising 38 *tons* of babies!

It is impossible to say from the graphs whether the remaining seasonal pattern of births is a result of some natural inbuilt seasonal 'clock', or whether it arises from deliberate attempts to plan families so as to avoid winter births. Data on the seasonal pattern of sexual offences, given in Chapter 7, throws some light on this question.

The seasonal pattern of births has remained quite consistent over the last decade. On the other hand, the pattern of stillbirths changed dramatically around 1979. I had data for stillbirths only on a quarterly basis, and the results are shown at the bottom of Figure 5.1. The number of stillbirths per 1,000 live births has fallen sharply over the years, from about 12 in 1974 to about 6 in 1984. The improvement has been most marked in what was previously the most risky period, namely the January to March quarter.

Marriages

I haven't corrected the marriages data for the number of days in the month. It is likely that the number of Saturdays is a more important factor; also, whether

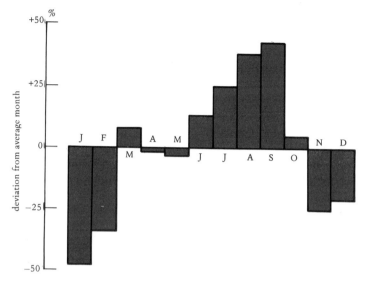

Fig. 5.2   Marriages

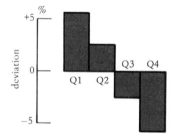

Fig. 5.3   Divorces (decrees made absolute)

Easter falls in March or April. Nevertheless, there is a very clear and very large seasonal effect, as would be expected (Figure 5.2). I wonder, though, whether the actual *shape* of the seasonal pattern is what you would have expected? I rather think that many people would have anticipated a higher peak around March and April. There *was* a particularly high level of 'beat-the-Budget' marriages in March 1975; otherwise Easter still falls consistently behind summer and early autumn in popularity by a very large margin.

Divorces

As with stillbirths, the data on divorces (Figure 5.3) are quarterly rather than monthly. In terms of decrees made absolute, there is a simple seasonal pattern in which the second half of the year is a mirror image of the first half.

Deaths

To analyse fully all of the comprehensive death statistics compiled by the Office of Population Censuses and Surveys would be a major research task in itself. Hence, most of this section is based on information for a single year, in the middle of the 10-year period which we are studying. The year chosen is 1979. Comparing quarterly data for this and other years shows that it can be taken as a reasonably typical year, although it did have below-average temperatures in January and February. As a check, I have plotted (in Figure 5.4a) the seasonal pattern for both 1979 and for 1983. The latter year was quite unusual. During that year, we experienced a very mild January but a very cold February. The consequential effects on mortality rates show up clearly in the diagram. 1983 will also be remembered for the long, hot summer: both July and August were unusually hot, dry and sunny. It looks as if the excessive heat may have brought forward some deaths to July which might otherwise not have occurred until the following month.

Even such an extreme year is not all that different from the more normal 1979. Consequently, I'm quite happy that 1979 data will provide a very good indication of the patterns which would be expected for other 'normal' years as well. Deaths rise from a low in August to a sharp peak in January, nearly 50 per cent higher than the August low.

Over the complete range of all ages, women seem to have a death rate relatively higher than men in the spring (Figure 5.4b). This may be explained at least partly by the different age profiles of men and women: on average the latter live about three years longer, so that they become an increasing proportion of the population as we go up the age range; and different age groups many have different seasonal mortality patterns. If we look at death rates just for those people in one age group – i.e. those already over 80 – we can see in Figure 5.5 that the graphs for men and women have identical shapes; the difference is that the scale for women is exactly double that for men because there are that many more women who reach that stage of maturity. (This is a fact of life which seems to cause consternation to the Equal Opportunities Commission; actuarial calculations inevitably show that women should receive a lower return than men on an annuity, but this is seen in some circles as sexist discrimination.)

There are three causes which account for by far the largest proportions of

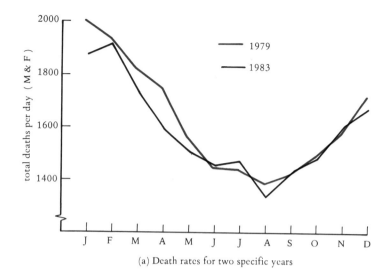

(a) Death rates for two specific years

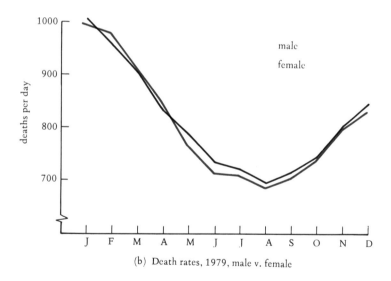

(b) Death rates, 1979, male v. female

Fig. 5.4   Death rates – summary

Crown copyright. Reproduced with permission from the Office of Population Censuses and Surveys.

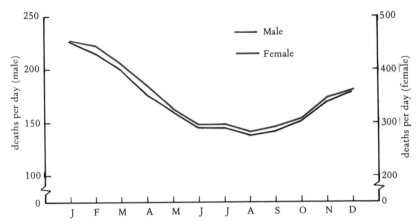

Fig. 5.5   Death rates – ages 80 and over

Crown copyright. Reproduced with permission from the Office of Population Censuses and Surveys.

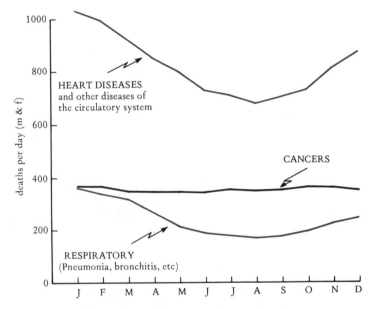

Fig. 5.6   The more common causes of death

Crown copyright. Reproduced with permission from the Office of Population Censuses and Surveys.

deaths. These are shown in Figure 5.6. Deaths from heart diseases and respiratory diseases closely follow the pattern already given for total deaths. Cancer-related deaths are quite different: there is no evidence of any significant seasonal effect. I wonder why this is? Perhaps it is because cancer

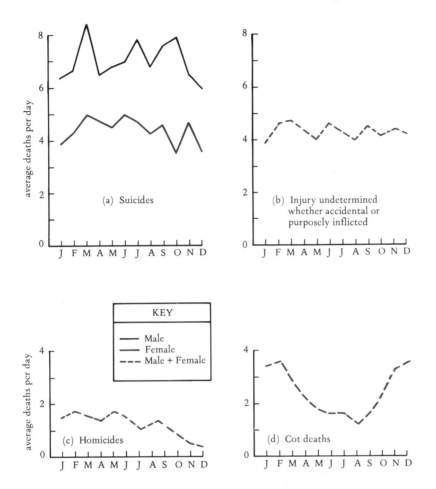

Fig. 5.7   Some of the more uncommon causes of death

Crown copyright. Reproduced with permission from the Office of Population Censuses and Surveys.

patients are more likely to complete their lives in hospitals, which have their own all-year-round climates?

In Figure 5.7, I have presented results for some of the less common causes of death. I should emphasize that, with such a small number of people involved, data for one specific year may not be completely representative, although they will give a good indication of the general shape of the seasonal pattern or (in some cases) non-pattern. Also, deaths which are not registered before 31 March of the following year are not included in the statistics. This *may* account for part, if not all, of the fall in the number of murders recorded in the later months of the year.

With the possible exception of a genuinely lower murder rate in the last quarter, the personally-inflicted causes of death show no obvious month-to-month variations. (In fact, if anything, the pattern is just the reverse of that for natural causes: for instance suicides seem to be lowest in the winter and highest in the middle of the year.) It is interesting to note the similarity with cancer deaths (Figure 5.6); the latter exhibit a steady month-to-month level, which is more typical of other man-made causes of death. Although we presumably *do* create the causes ourselves by smoking, pollution and the use of chemicals, I nevertheless found it very surprising that the ultimate effect of these abuses is not reflected in higher death rates in winter.

There has been much publicity about a most tragic cause of infant mortality called 'sudden infant death syndrome' or, more popularly, 'cot deaths'. Much to the distress of the parents concerned, there has been controversy as to whether these deaths are entirely from 'natural' causes. I suggest that the seasonal pattern of such deaths leaves no doubt at all, despite the small numbers involved, that this tragic phenomenon is entirely natural: the seasonal pattern is almost precisely in line with that of other natural causes of death.

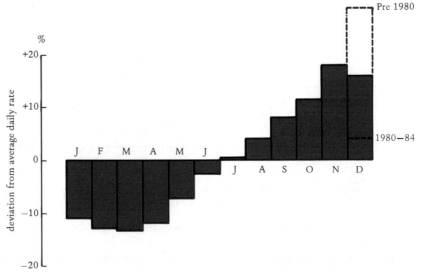

Fig. 5.8   Fatal road casualties – seasonal pattern

So far, we have looked at one particular year. In the case of road deaths (Figure 5.8) I *have* started with a 10-year history, using the figures which are published separately in the *Monthly Digest of Statistics*. These figures produce a remarkably clear picture of a rising trend from early spring up to late autumn. A close look at the individual figures for each month shows that this seasonal pattern is very consistent indeed from one year to another, with one exception. Up to 1979, the upward trend continued, and indeed accelerated, beyond November into December. Since 1980, December has been little worse than the average for the year; indeed, in 1981 there was actually a substantially below-average level of road deaths in December. These December results presumably reflect the varying degrees of success of the 'don't-drink-and-drive' campaigns around Christmas time. As a rough guess, I estimate that the effect since 1980 has been to reduce the December death toll by about 20 per cent (which means a reduction of about 100 deaths each year); the effect in December 1981 alone, compared with the earlier years 1975 to 1980, must have been over 200 lives saved.

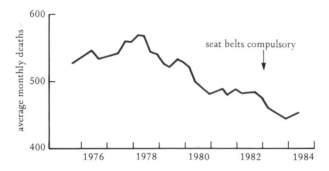

Fig. 5.9   Longer-term trend in fatal road accidents

The introduction of seat belts might reduce the general level of fatal accidents, but is unlikely to have affected the seasonal pattern. Figure 5.9 shows the long-term trend; I have indicated on this graph the date at which the wearing of seat belts became compulsory. It is not altogether clear just what effect this has had. The number of fatalities has decreased since that time, but it had been decreasing anyway for a few years. In those earlier years there was an extensive publicity campaign to encourage people to wear seat belts voluntarily, and it does look as if the various measures – persuasion and legislation – have had a very significant effect over the years.

We shall move on, in the next chapter, to the rather less morbid subject of keeping well whilst still alive.

6   Health

A useful measure of the general state of people's health (or, rather, ill health) is the number of prescriptions issued. The seasonal pattern is given in Figure 6.1. Two features stand out in this chart: first, the peak period for sickness is February/March: secondly, the summer holiday period is a relatively healthy time. The latter observation will come as no surprise; on the other hand, it is popularly believed that the peak period for illness comes rather earlier in the winter than it really does.

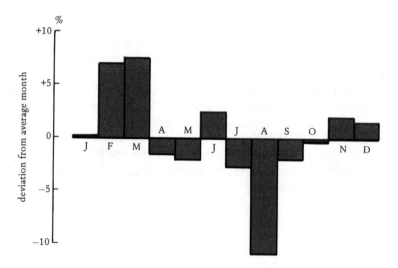

Fig. 6.1   Number of prescriptions per day

Another surprise (to me) was to find that, on average, one person in two is issued with a prescription each month. Quite a lot of people have regular monthly prescriptions, of course; this means that the real seasonal pattern of sickness is actually even more pronounced than that illustrated in Figure 6.1.

Another way of looking at sickness is to analyse absenteeism from work. I was able to analyse such a set of figures only for one particular group of people, with the results shown in Figure 6.2. This shows some interesting similarities and also some differences when compared to the number of prescriptions issued. Most obviously, February/March is the worst time for sickness, whether measured by the number of prescriptions or by absence from work. Meanwhile, in December and January, there is a higher incidence of presumably minor ailments which are not serious enough to keep their sufferers away from work. The opposite is observed for August: reduced absence from work doesn't really match the fall-off in the issue of prescriptions.

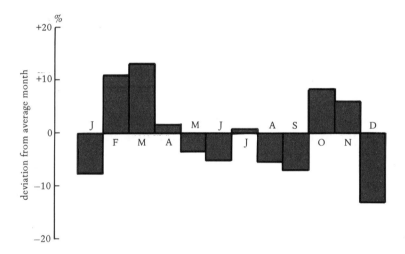

Fig. 6.2   Sickness and absenteeism – % of available time

The greatest puzzle about these patterns is that they are somewhat different from the seasonal pattern of deaths. I would have anticipated that the conditions which engender high levels of sickness would be precisely the same conditions which would cause high death rates. This is not entirely so.

The data for both dental services and eyesight tests are published regularly, but only on a quarterly basis. The results of analysing these data are shown in Figure 6.3. The patterns are similar to each other, but the variations are more

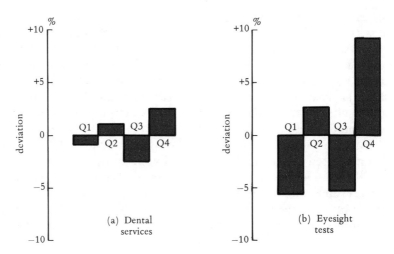

Fig. 6.3   Specialist health services

pronounced in the case of eyesight tests. The latter are undertaken very largely at the discretion of the individual; this is less true of dental services, of course, as many of these visits arise from immediate problems calling for immediate action. Insofar as people *do* have a choice in these things, they clearly prefer to receive these services in the last quarter of the year and, to a lesser extent, the second quarter.

So, if you want to minimize the time you spend in waiting rooms, the answer is to book your treatment for the first and/or third quarters of the year.

7 Crime

As with opticians and dentists, the statistics on offences are published quarterly. By coincidence (at least, I presume that it is coincidence!) the quarterly pattern for crime shown in Figure 7.1a is very similar to that for medical services.

A total of 3½ million notifiable offences were recorded by the police in England and Wales in 1984. (This represents an average of 4 per person in a life-time!) They were made up as follows:

	%
Theft and handling stolen goods	52
Burglary	26
Criminal damage	14
Fraud and forgery	4
Violence against the person	3
Robbery	1
Sexual offences	½

Figure 7.1 illustrates the seasonal patterns, not only for total crime, but also for the three most common individual categories, which in total account for some 90 per cent of notifiable offences. These individual patterns are broadly similar to that for total crime, with the main exception that burglaries are very much more prevalent in the winter.

In sharp contrast, the less common offences (Figure 7.2) exhibit quite different patterns to the total and, by and large, to each other.

The pattern of sexual offences follows broadly the same pattern as for conceptions – compare Figure 7.2d with what Figure 5.1b would look like if

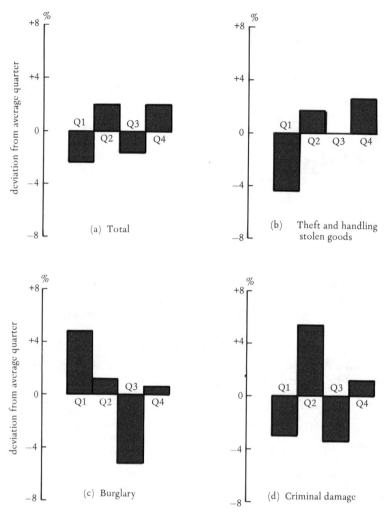

Fig. 7.1   The more common criminal offences

drawn on a quarterly basis. The same kind of pattern – low in the first quarter and peaking in the third quarter – is also evident for crimes of violence against the person.

The most violent crimes – murders – were mentioned in Chapter 5 in the analysis of deaths by various causes. There was some evidence that the number of murders is low in the final quarter of the year. There are some very long-term cycles in murders which are actually much more interesting than the seasonal patterns. Cesare Marchetti, of the International Institute for Applied Systems Analysis in Vienna, has found some very long cycles in US

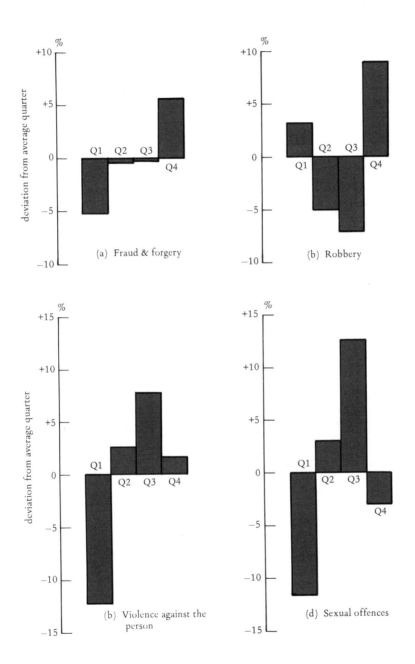

Fig. 7.2   The less common criminal offences

murders which seem to be related to a long-wave economic cycle of some 50-plus years' duration (the 'Kondriatieff Cycle'). For instance, in a period of prosperity, there is a tendency for murders to be by shooting; in a recession, there is a much greater tendency for murders to be by stabbing.

In Chapter 12 we shall see the seasonal pattern of television viewing; there is *no* evidence from that pattern that television has a significant effect on the general seasonal pattern of violence in society: violence is actually highest when television viewing is at its lowest.

If television is really the cause of increased violence in society, then we would expect the seasonal pattern of violence to have changed as television has become the all-pervasive means of communication. Going back to 1976 – which is as far back as the statistics are recorded in the *Monthly Digest* – I can see no evidence at all of such a relevant change in the seasonal pattern.

One thing that *has* happened is that the *number* of violent crimes has increased substantially. However, that trend has been accompanied by an increasing tendency for such crimes to be committed in the *low* season for TV viewing. Rather than blame television for the increased violence, it would be easier to suggest that violence in the winter months is actually *relatively lower* than it used to be, as people spend more of their winter evenings glued to the television screen.

8 Employment and incomes

We now come to one of the most important questions of the day, namely, jobs.

Firstly, the availability of jobs. Figure 8.1 shows the seasonal patterns of job vacancies notified to Job Centres but unfilled at the first week of each month. This is probably the best picture of the demand for labour in the economy. It reflects very closely the pattern of business optimism which we shall see later, in Chapter 16; i.e. a major peak in the spring and a secondary peak in the autumn.

This figure actually gives a better picture of labour demand than does that for unemployment, which is also shown in Figure 8.1.

Actually, from January to August the seasonal pattern of unemployment is a mirror image of the pattern for job vacancies. Then, in September and October, we see the effect of the sudden influx of school leavers. The December results are initially somewhat surprising: unemployment falls slightly even though the demand for labour also falls. I can only think that this has something to do with the seasonal Christmas trade: either there is a substantial increase in jobs which are not advertised via Job Centres, or many jobs are being advertised but are taken up very quickly, leaving only a small number of unfilled vacancies on the day of the count. There is also a considerable amount of overtime worked in December, as we shall see in a minute.

The seasonal patterns of overtime and short-time working contain some surprises. Before we look at them, it is worth spending a moment or two looking at the long-term patterns, shown in Figure 8.2, exhibited by the moving averages (note the logarithmic scales). We would expect that in a recessionary period (e.g. 1980–2) overtime working would decrease and short-time working increase; the reverse would be expected in a boom (e.g.

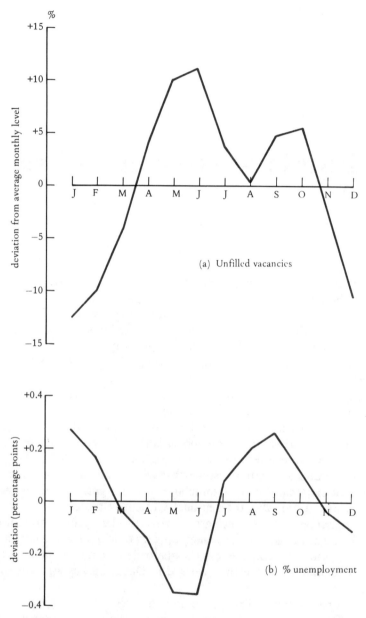

Fig. 8.1   **Employment**

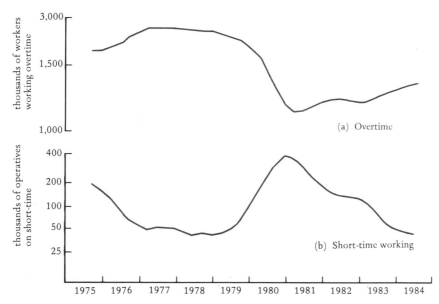

Fig. 8.2   Long-term patterns in overtime and short-time working

1977−8). This is precisely what happens in practice: the overtime graph is a mirror image of the short-time working graph.

I thought it useful to introduce this diagram, just to assure ourselves that our intuition is right. Because, when we come to the seasonal patterns, that same intuition doesn't tell the whole story. Those patterns are shown in Figure 8.3. The two charts are by no means mirror images of each other. It *is* true of December and January: December is the peak month for overtime and short-time working is low; overtime then falls off in January and short-time working increases rapidly. On the other hand, the mid-summer holiday period is one in which *both* overtime *and* short-time working are very low. This apparent anomaly does actually have a logic of its own. Total business activity is at a low ebb generally in August, as we shall see in Chapter 19. Many firms react to generally weak market conditions by having a complete holiday shutdown in August, so avoiding lay-offs and short-time working.

The seasonal pattern of earnings is shown in Figure 8.4. This diagram indicates the effects of the annual pay 'round', which reaches a peak in June or July. Earnings also include the seasonal effects of overtime working, and this causes a secondary peak in the earnings pattern in November and December. Unlike the factors discussed earlier in this chapter, the month-to-month variations for earnings are quite small; the total range is only 2 per cent. These small differences are, however, quite consistent and statistically significant.

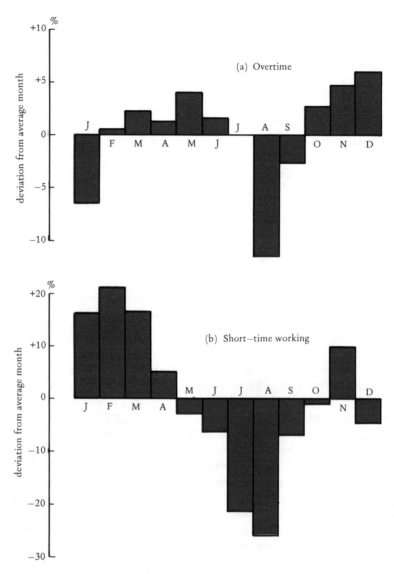

Fig. 8.3   Overtime and short-time working

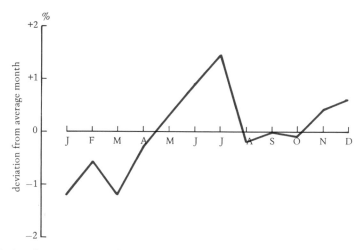

Fig. 8.4   Average earnings

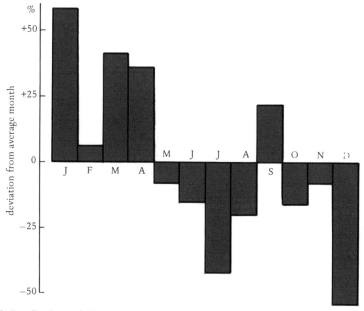

Fig. 8.5   Industrial stoppages

When we look at strikes (Figure 8.5), we are once again looking at some very large monthly variations. The figures relate to the month in which a dispute *starts*; if a dispute continues into subsequent months, it is *not* included in the data for those months.

The difficulty in analysing this series is that it is dominated by a few very high values. This remains so even when we work with the logarithms of the actual data. The month-to-month differences are statistically significant, although you should not take too literally the precise shape of the pattern.

Nevertheless, there are some consistent features. The number of stoppages exceeded the moving average level in 8 out of 9 Januaries and fell below the moving average in all 9 Decembers. Had it not been for a very high number of stoppages in August 1979, the average figure for August would have been much lower – more in line with the July rate.

It is worth nothing that (with the exception of the January peak), the pattern is very similar to many which we shall see in Part III. Strike activity tends to go up and down in parallel with business confidence; a peak in March, falling off in mid-summer, a secondary peak in the autumn and finally falling off rapidly at the end of the year. Strike activity apparently has no serious adverse effect on business confidence; on the contrary, both strikes and business confidence seem to go hand-in-hand with many other aspects of business activity.

9 Retail prices

The retail price index is constructed by averaging price changes for an extensive 'shopping basket' of goods. You may be interested in just what the components of this shopping basket are: the various categories are shown in Figure 9.1.

They fall into two broad groups: food and non-food. It would obviously have been possible to analyse the seasonal patterns for any of the individual components, but to give the general picture I have limited the results to food, non-food and total sales. The seasonal patterns are shown in Figure 9.2.

The magnitude of the variations is quite small, but nevertheless the results are statistically significant. From 1975 to 1984, prices pursued a more-or-less steady upwards path, with relatively minor variations due to the development of the business cycle. As a result, the monthly variations from the moving averages are fairly consistent from year to year. For instance, for the general index of prices, the January, February and March deviations were negative for every single year from 1978 to 1984. Similarly, the April to August period produced only 6 negative deviations out of 45 values. In other words the general shape of the seasonal pattern is very consistent from one year to another. Nevertheless, although it is consistent, it is not very large for either food or non-food items.

A slightly larger variation occurs in the food category. The 2 per cent difference between the spring peak and autumn minimum is very largely due to the much more pronounced seasonal variations in the price of things like eggs, fruit and vegetables. We shall look in Chapter 21 at the kind of price changes that can occur over the year as far as fresh foods are concerned. The charts in Chapter 21 are based on US data, but they nevertheless give a good impression of the kind of substantial seasonal variations which can occur.

The main groups		The main food items		Housing		Transport & vehicles	
Food	19%	Meat & bacon	25%	Mortgage interest	30%	Purchase of vehicles	35%
Alcoholic drink	7½%	Dairy produce	18%	Rates (inc. water)	29%	Petrol & oil	32%
Tobacco	4%	Bread, cakes, cereals etc.	13%	Rent	20%	Maintenance	10%
Durable goods	6½%	Vegetables	10%	Repairs & maintenance	17%	Insurance	6%
Clothing & footwear	7½%	Sugar, jam	8%	Other	3%	Licences	6%
Misc. goods	8%	Tea, coffee & other drinks	6%			Other costs	2%
Services	6%	Fruit	6%			Fares	9%
Meals out	4½%	Pet food	6%				
Housing	15%	Fish	3%				
Fuel & light	6½%	Others	4%				
Transport & vehicles	15½%						
Total	100%	Total	100%	Total	100%	Total	100%

Fig. 9.1 General index of retail prices – the constituents of the standard 'shopping basket'

Note: Totals do not always add up to exactly 100% because of rounding errors.

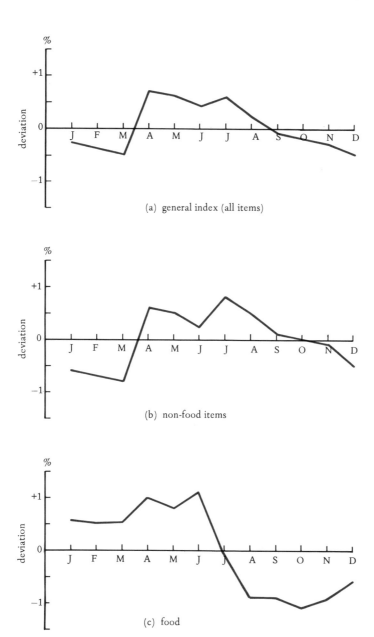

(a) general index (all items)

(b) non-food items

(c) food

Fig. 9.2   Retail prices

In the next chapter, we look at the *volume* of sales for various kinds of products. You might have guessed that high seasonal prices would correspond to months of high seasonal demand. Whilst it is true that February and March are characterized by both low prices and low demand, there is otherwise no obvious connection between seasonal prices and seasonal demand. In fact, price increases are more significant at mid-year, when sales are somewhat *below* average; conversely, they are low in December when sales are really buoyant.

10   Retail sales

Just as we started the last chapter by looking at the components of retail *prices*, we shall now look at the make-up of retail *sales*; this is shown in Figure 10.1. This table is based on figures for the total annual sales of the various categories of retailers.

For the UK economy as a whole, the total of all sales by all retailers is given in official statistics for 1984 as £80,400 million (i.e. £80.4 billion). By coincidence, if we assume that an average family consists of just under 3 people, then each average family purchases in a week just about one-billionth of total national annual sales. So, if we drop the 'billion' off the national totals we have a good estimate of average weekly expenditure for a family. This is almost certainly a figure which you will find easier to understand than a figure of £80 billion.

Several of the items listed are, of course, not typical weekly purchases. Whereas we may well recognize the £25 per week spent at the grocers (mainly supermarkets), it is less easy to relate to the £4.50 per week spent on furniture, as this may really represent no more than one item a year. Nevertheless, the table should give you a good picture of the relative amounts spent with each type of retailer.

I've chosen just a few of the possibly more interesting components for analysis from the full list in Figure 10.1. (For much greater detail on this subject, see *Retail Planning and Seasonal Forecasts for 1987 and 1988* by J. de Somogyi and R.J. Hall.) Before looking at these components, however, we shall first look at two of the broad categories which correspond to the patterns described in the previous chapter, on prices. Figure 10.2 shows the seasonal patterns for total sales and for sales by food retailers. These patterns are roughly similar: i.e. the most pronounced feature is the way in which they rise

Food		Clothing and Footwear		Household goods		Other non-food		Mixed retailers	
Grocers	£25.30	Women's wear	£3.90	Furniture	£4.50	Confectioners & tobacconists	£6.60	Large Departmental	£11.30
Butchers	£2.40	Men's and boys' wear	£1.50	Electrical	£2.90	Off-licences	£2.00	Mail order	£2.70
Dairymen	£1.90	Footwear	£1.80	Do-it-yourself	£1.70	Booksellers & stationers	£1.10	Others	£0.90
Greengrocers & fruiterers	£1.10			TV etc	£1.30	Chemists (Excluding NHS)	£1.10		
Bakers	£0.80			Hardware	£1.30	Jewellers	£1.10		
Fishmongers	£0.20			Electricity showrooms	£0.60	Toys	£0.90		
				Gas showrooms	£0.30	Others	£1.40		
	£31.80		£7.10		£12.50		£14.10		£14.90

For an average family of 2.9 people – total purchases from all retailers = £80.40 per week
For the whole of the UK – total retail sales = £80,400 million in 1984
(Seasonal patterns are given for those totals and individual groups of retailers shown in red.)

Fig. 10.1 Summary of retail sales

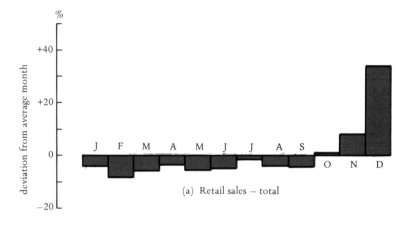

(a) Retail sales – total

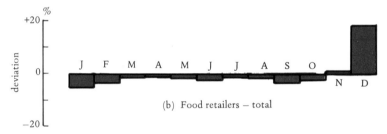

(b) Food retailers – total

Fig. 10.2 Total retail sales

to a very sharp peak in December. Sales in that month are about 40 per cent above those for most other months in the year. This is one of the most pronounced of all the seasonal features which affect business. You might well imagine that businessmen would be rubbing their hands in glee with all that money flowing into the tills. To anticipate something which comes later, I have to say that December is one of the months when the average businessman is at his most pessimistic.

Financing retail purchases by hire purchase

There is one other factor which we shall consider before looking at retail sales in a little more detail. Figure 10.3 shows the seasonal pattern in new credit extended by retailers to finance some of the purchases which we shall be studying. The picture is understandably similar in outline to the seasonal sales pattern, but it differs quite a lot in detail. In the first place, the largest increase in credit actually comes a month *earlier* than the sales peak. December is still a buoyant month for hire purchase, but not in proportion to the total level of sales in that month: Christmas presents are not often bought on hire purchase!

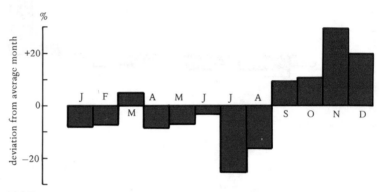

Fig. 10.3   Hire purchase – new credit extended by retailers

More puzzling is the significant rise in hire purchase in March, a month in which retail sales are below average; and the fall in July when the sales are not at all bad. The March increase in credit was a very consistent phenomenon until recent years and will have been associated with purchases made just ahead of the Budget. In the most recent years (1983 and 1984) this pre-Budget credit spree disappeared, and there was a correspondingly higher uptake of new credit in January.

The sharp (and completely consistent) fall-off in new credit in July has no such immediately obvious explanation. Sales generally in July are not at all depressed, especially of the kind of things (household goods) which might be expected to be financed by hire purchase. It looks as if many of the people who would normally be buying on hire purchase are, in July and August, more interested in their annual holiday than in taking on more debt. The relatively good month which retailers experience in July will have something to do with the summer sales; a high proportion of these transactions must be financed by means other than hire purchase.

Clothing sales

The first of the individual components which we shall look at is clothing and footwear; the results are given in Figure 10.4.

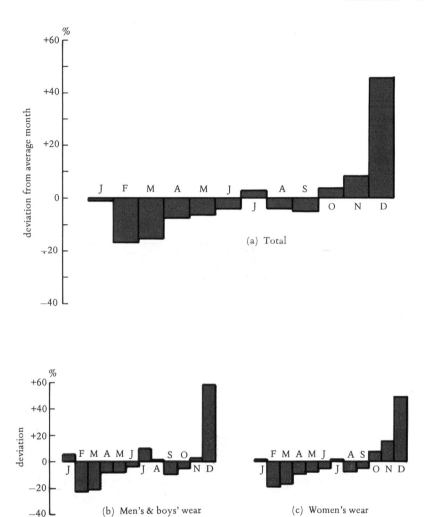

Fig. 10.4 Clothing and footwear sales

The seasonal pattern adheres very closely to that for total retail sales; the magnitudes of the deviations are slightly larger, but the general shape is very similar. The one interesting difference is that clothing and footwear do rather better than average in the January and summer sales.

A closer look at this phenomenon shows that it is much more pronounced with men than with women. The latter are more prone to add to their wardrobes in the period leading up to Christmas; the evidently more mercenary men are more inclined to wait for a bargain.

Household goods

The effect of the sales in January and July is also clearly seen in the chart for household goods (Figure 10.5); the January peak is particularly pronounced.

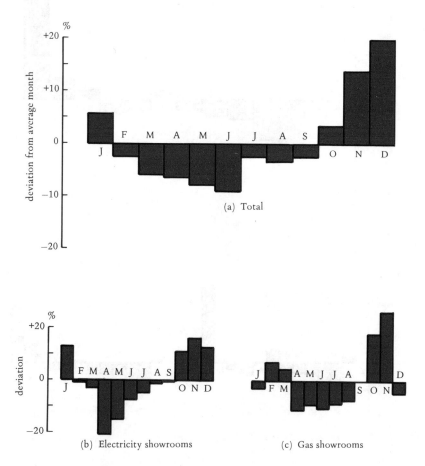

Fig. 10.5   Sales of household goods

You may like to ponder on the different seasonal patterns which are illustrated for two popular High Street chains, namely the electricity and gas showrooms. Of all the separate retail sectors which I analysed, the gas showrooms were the only outlets for which sales in December were actually *below* the yearly average. This low rate of sales spills over into January, a time when the electricity showrooms are very busy. Gas showroom sales then pick up well in February and March, which is again a rather unusual pattern.

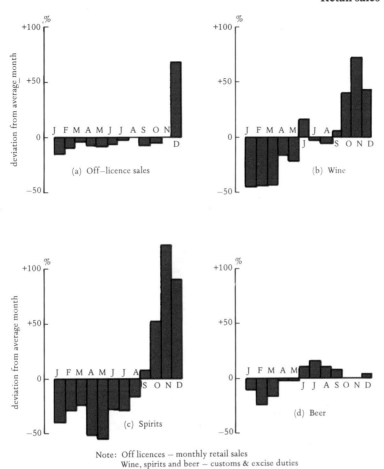

Note: Off licences — monthly retail sales
Wine, spirits and beer — customs & excise duties

Fig. 10.6   Alcoholic drinks

Off-licences

Off-licence sales are shown in Figure 10.6. The seasonal pattern is dominated by the Christmas trade.

The published retail sales figures don't subdivide total sales into separate figures for wines, spirits and beer. However, we can obtain a very good picture of these components from the figures for customs and excise duties. The timing of the receipt of duties will not correspond exactly to the timing of the retail sales, but the figures do give us a good comparison between the various types of alcoholic drink. The patterns shown in Figure 10.6 will not be at all surprising; it's just the magnitude of the seasonal factors which may be new to you. As far as spirits are concerned, about half of total annual

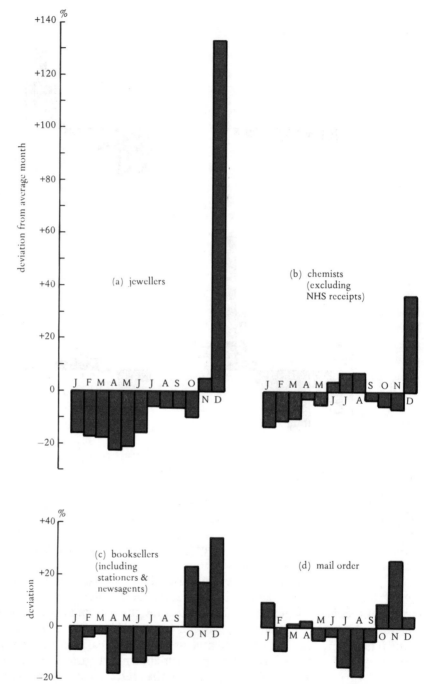

Fig. 10.7 Sales by other retailers

sales occur in the last three months of the year.

The pattern for wine is quite similar; meanwhile the patterns for both wine and spirits differ completely from that for beer. The latter exhibits a relatively modest peak in the summer months which mirrors a decline in the winter. The minor peak at Christmas is perhaps surprisingly small.

'Other' retailers

Those of you who read Chapter 3 will be very familiar already with the seasonal pattern of jewellery sales. You have seen the graph of actual monthly sales; Figure 10.7a shows how this translates into a seasonal pattern. The December peak is one of the largest single monthly factors which I have come across in this study.

There are some other series which show equally large or even larger peaks. One of these occurs in one of the very first time series which I was ever asked to look at, namely the sales of fireworks. I remember this study with great pleasure, as it 'sparked off' an interest in the whole question of forecasting.

Chemists and booksellers both show the December peak, although to nothing like the same extent as jewellers. Otherwise, each series has its own individual characteristics.

Mail order, too, produces a very individual pattern. The need to allow 28 days for delivery shows up very clearly inasmuch as the Christmas peak actually occurs in November. It is also interesting to see that mail order companies, just as much as other retailers, have their own January sales; they, also, do a substantial amount of business at that time.

Our review in retail sales has included some groups, such as household goods, which represent large capital purchases rather than weekly consumables. None of these, however, represents such a large capital outlay as the purchase of a car. This is the subject of the next chapter.

TECHNICAL NOTE (A)

Retail sales data are published in the *Monthly Digest of Statistics* in index form. In recent years, this index has been based on 1980 = 100. However, the basis has been changed fairly regularly and sometimes the precise definitions of the various categories change. In practice, I found it a fairly easy matter to 'splice together' the figures for the years 1979 to 1984, which included data with three separate bases: 1976 = 100; 1978 = 100 and 1980 = 100. The seasonal patterns are so consistent from year to year that it was both unnecessary and unwise to go back to earlier years, for which the index was based on 1971 = 100 and the make-up of each sector may have changed somewhat.

The published data are based on weekly averages, so that there was no need to correct for the different lengths of each month.

TECHNICAL NOTE (B)

The results for excise duties on wines and spirits are based on just a few years' data, namely 1982 to 1984. As with retail sales, this doesn't matter at all since the seasonal effects are very consistent.

The reason why I have not included pre-1981 data may itself be of interest. Up to that time, the published figures were for wines and spirits in total; they were not recorded separately. The subsequent subdivision into two separate components typifies a growth business. The subdivision of wines and spirits into the two separate components was a good indication (if it was not already obvious) of the growing interest in wine.

Incidentally, you can sometimes spot good growth markets even before they are given a separate category of their own. A valuable piece of advice which I was once given is to delve into the 'not elsewhere specified' sections of official statistics if you want to spot tomorrow's winners.

11 Cars

With the exception of a house, the purchase of a car is for most people their largest single item of expenditure. You will be well aware of the fact that many people buying new cars wait for the new registration letter to appear in August; Figure 11.1a illustrates the size of this August peak. You will also see how sales in July – and to a lesser extent in June – are depressed whilst people wait for the new registration year.

A secondary feature is that some people wait, not for the new registration year, but for the new *calendar* year. This means that sales are depressed towards the end of the year, but rise in January, a little time ahead of the more 'natural' peak in the spring.

It would be reasonable to expect that the same kind of seasonal pattern would be found in the payment of vehicle excise duties. This is, in fact, not the case. Figure 11.1b shows the seasonal pattern derived from published data on the receipt of vehicle excise duties. Now these excise duties are, of course, payable on many more vehicles than just private cars; nevertheless, it is something of a surprise not to find the August peak reflected in this lower diagram. Incidentally, I should emphasize that Figure 11(b) measures the *revenue* from licences rather than the *number* of licences. As a consequence, at least part of the March peak (and February trough) will be due to the fact that the licence fee tends to go up in March.

With any change to October as the starting point for new registrations, I'm afraid that you will need to use your own judgement as to the pattern in subsequent years!

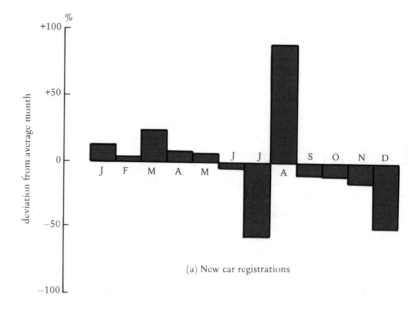

(a) New car registrations

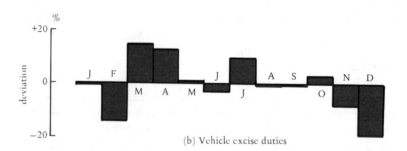

(b) Vehicle excise duties

Fig. 11.1   New cars

12 Holidays and entertainment

In this chapter, I shall just give a little of the flavour of the subject by taking a few specific examples.

We shall start with a form of entertainment which is very much less popular than it used to be many years ago, namely visits to the cinema; the seasonal pattern is illustrated in Figure 12.1. I wonder how many of you, when answering the quiz in Chapter 2, agreed that August was the peak month? It is, as you can see, and by a substantial margin. Not all of the holiday hours are spent basking in the sun! (In fact, much of the August peak is caused by holiday-makers escaping from the rain.) The other possible surprise in this picture is the relatively low level of cinema attendances in the early part of the winter.

The decline in popularity of the cinema has gone hand-in-hand with a huge increase in television viewing. The red line in Figure 12.2 shows the monthly variations in viewing hours, measured from the average figure of 5 hours per day for an average household.

The shape of this curve is probably exactly what you would have expected. Less obvious (and not illustrated in the diagram) are the changing preferences for BBC and ITV. The BBC's share of the total audience has tended to be higher during the period May to July; there has been a sharp swing towards commercial television in the autumn.

Figure 12.2 also shows the seasonal pattern of payments for television licences. With the exception of February/March, this pattern follows that of the viewing figures, but in a more exaggerated way: it provides a much more dramatic illustration of how attention turns to television as winter approaches. The February/March anomaly is associated with the annual price increase which we have come to expect at the time of the Budget: the March

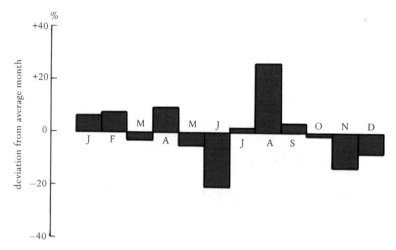

Fig. 12.1   Cinema admissions

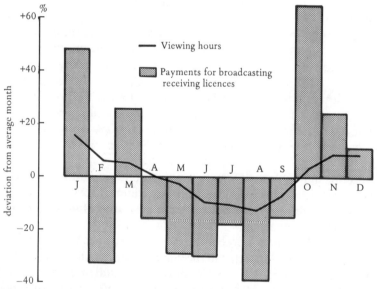

Fig. 12.2   Television viewing

increase partly reflects this price factor directly; it may also indicate that there is a mini-rush to renew licences in early March, ahead of that price increase.

I have also used receipts of duties to illustrate the seasonal variation in betting and gaming (Figure 12.3). There is a surge of interest in the autumn and this then falls off in the winter months. This decline in the winter will

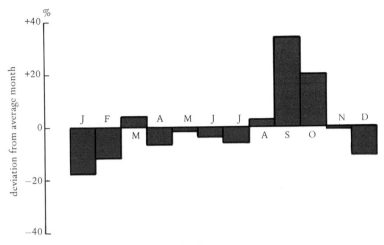

Fig. 12.3   Betting and gaming duties

include the effect of the cancellation of a relatively large number of horse-racing events during those months.

Turning now to holidays, three different patterns are illustrated in Figure 12.4:

- the numbers of UK residents going abroad;
- the numbers of overseas visitors coming to Britain;
- the total number of passengers carried by UK airlines.

The patterns are all very similar and unsurprising: most people like to take their summer holiday in the summer! Rather more British than overseas holidaymakers leave their holidays until September.

The monthly variations in airline passengers are much less pronounced than the variations in holidays abroad. The reason for this, of course, is that the airline data include a substantial number of business travellers; their journeys are spread more evenly throughout the year. You can, in fact, see from Figure 12.4 how the number of business travellers falls off sharply in August: the airline pattern does not reflect the very sharp August peak of holidaymaking.

In the last few chapters, we have looked at seasonal patterns in the way people spend their money, whether it be in shops, on new cars or on leisure pursuits. We shall move on now to look at patterns in some forms of saving. I have included housing in between the 'spending' and the 'savings' chapters, as house purchase can be regarded *either* as something you spend money on *or* as an investment (or, indeed, as both). Also, a look at housing will lead us

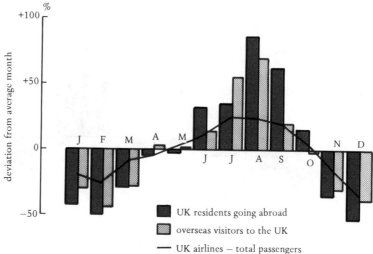

Fig. 12.4   Holidays and travel

naturally into one of the most popular and widespread forms of saving, namely building society investments.

TECHNICAL NOTE

A simplified approach was used to plot the patterns for holidaymakers, both to and from the UK. The official statistics are given in both 'un-adjusted' and 'seasonally adjusted' forms. I simply calculated the seasonal patterns from the ratios of these two sets of figures for 1984.

---

13 Housing and building societies

Buying a house represents, for most of us, at one and the same time our largest purchase and our largest investment. Housing also has a rather special role in the national economy, inasmuch as it is backed by its own system of finance. The building society is a feature of English-speaking countries; elsewhere, there is not the same clear distinction between borrowing for house purchase and borrowing for anything else. In recent years, the distinction has become increasingly blurred, even in Britain, as banks have moved into the house purchase field and building societies have come to anticipate an increasingly wider financial role for themselves.

Nevertheless, the building society is still the first place that very many people think of, whether it be to take out a mortgage or as a home for their savings. So, in this chapter, I have linked housing and building societies together, notwithstanding the changes that are under way. The two subjects together represent a natural bridge between chapters on spending and on investments.

The idea of a house as a safe 'investment' is ingrained into our thinking, after so many years of inflation. Almost everyone assumes that house prices will always increase, although those of you with very long memories will know that that need not always be the case. In fact, your memory doesn't have to go back to the 1930s; you may remember that average house prices actually fell slightly for a time during the recession of 1981/2; they ended 1981 at a slightly lower level than at the start of that year.

What we shall be looking at, of course, are not these longer-term trends, but the month-to-month variations. Before looking at housing and house prices, we shall start by looking at building society finance.

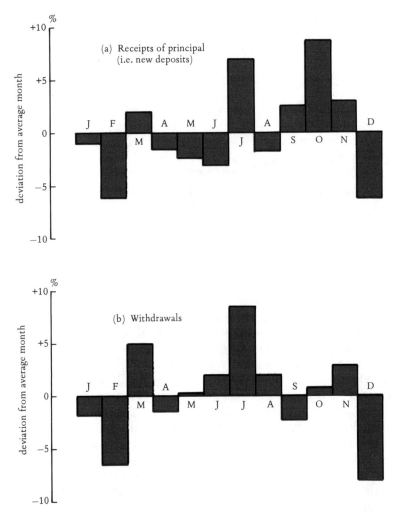

Fig. 13.1   Building societies – receipts and withdrawals

Investments in building societies

Figure 13.1 shows the monthly patterns of money paid into and taken out of building society accounts. The surprising feature of this figure is that the two charts – new deposits and withdrawals of existing deposits – are *not* mirror images of each other. You would probably have imagined, as I did, that the months in which investors are putting most money *into* building society accounts would also be the months in which they are taking little *out*. This is not so, which partly reflects the extent to which money is moved *between* societies, chasing the best interest rates. In any one month, the level of withdrawals is about three-quarters of the 'new' money invested; however, what is 'new' money for one society will include money which is a 'withdrawal' for one of its rivals.

The monthly variations are quite large, but initially show no obvious or logical pattern. To take a specific example, we might have expected withdrawals to be higher than they are in December, in order to finance Christmas shopping; probably the last thing we would have expected is to find that December is the month with the *lowest* level of withdrawals. This seems to be associated with the point made in the previous paragraph: withdrawals made with the object of re-investing in some other society (or some other form of security) look as if they fall off very sharply in December.

When we start to look more closely at the figures, the apparently inexplicable pattern begins to make more sense. The key is the seasonal pattern of interest payments credited to accounts. These are particularly high in June and December. Relative to the *difference* between deposits and withdrawals, interest payments have a profound (indeed, dominating) effect on the seasonal pattern.

Figure 13.2a shows the pattern for the 'net increase in shares and deposits outstanding', by which is meant the net effect of new deposits, withdrawals and interest payments. This shows the very strong effects of the half-yearly interest payments. (Note the differences in the scale of Figures 13.1 and 13.2a.)

There are secondary, intermediate peaks at the end of the intervening quarters, i.e. in March and September, but these are masked by the other monthly variations (in deposits and withdrawals). What I have done in Figure 13.2b is to show the net increase as a 3-month moving average. (For instance, the January result is shown as the average of the actual results for December, January and February.) In this way each month's average includes the actual result for one of the half-year or quarterly interest peaks. This goes some way to smoothing out the effects of the interest payment pattern.

The final step in this analysis is to reproduce Figure 13.2b upside down as shown in Figure 13.2c. In this way, a *peak* in the chart represents a *low* point for the net increase in deposits.

I have done this for a particular reason, in anticipation of many of the results which we shall be seeing in Part III. We shall see that very many series, in economics and business life, exhibit the kind of seasonal pattern shown by the dotted curve superimposed on Figure 13.2c. Indeed, the identification of such a pervasive 'M' shaped pattern is a key feature of subsequent chapters. The intriguing feature of the building society pattern is that it has had to be *inverted* in order to show this pattern. Anticipating what comes later, UK interest rates tend to be seasonally low in March/April and September/October; there is a corresponding increase in the purchases of (and

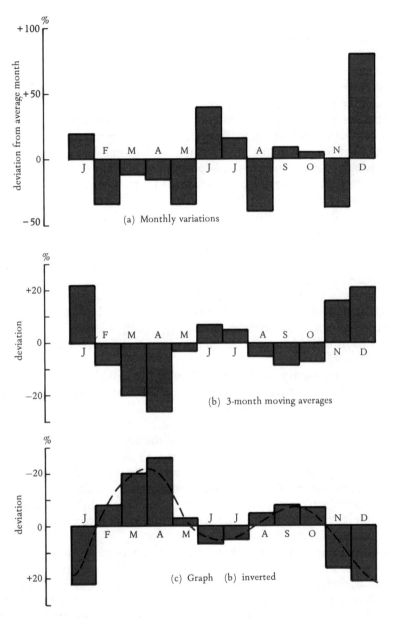

Fig. 13.2   **Building societies – net increase in shares and deposits**

value of) interest-rate-sensitive investments such as shares at those times, most especially in the spring.

What started off as an apparently arbitrary seasonal pattern is now beginning to make sense. When interest rates are seasonally low (e.g. March/April), money is attracted into investments (such as shares and bonds) which rise in value as interest rates decline; at such times, the value of leaving money in a building society declines, since there is no increase in capital value to compensate for the lower rate of interest. The reverse happens as interest rates rise, when building societies become an increasingly attractive and safe home for surplus funds. These periods (winter and summer) are also characterized by relative inertia in investors, as we shall see in Chapter 17; so, they are periods in which investors are quite happy to leave their money in building society accounts.

Housing

So far we have looked at the money invested in building societies. The other side of the coin is the use of these funds for house purchase.

The seasonal pattern of building society advances is illustrated in Figure 13.3. Two charts are given, one for the *number* of advances and the other for the *amount* of money advanced. Not surprisingly, the two patterns are almost identical. The winter period, December to February, is one in which interest in house purchase is at a relatively low ebb.

This pattern is reproduced very closely in the seasonal pattern of house *prices*, as shown at the bottom of Figure 13.3. The magnitude of the variations in prices is very much less, but the shapes are almost the same. The price pattern even picks up the minor dip in mortgage advances in September.

If the magnitudes of the seasonal variations (in mortgage advances and prices) had been more similar, it would have been difficult to differentiate between cause and effect: i.e. are house prices lower in certain months because less mortgage money is being made available, or does less money need to be made available because prices are lower? However, given the fact that mortgage advances vary by an order of magnitude more than do prices, then it is clear that it is the supply of mortgage funds which influences house prices, rather than vice versa.

Net effect on building society funds

We have seen that money going *into* building society accounts and going *out* to finance house purchases both exhibit strong seasonal patterns. The final question we shall look at in this chapter is: what is the net effect of all of these movements on the building societies?

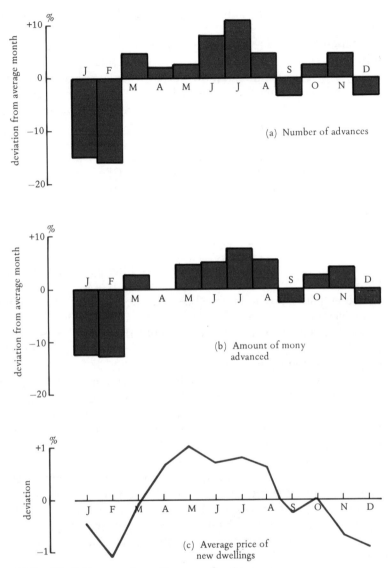

Fig. 13.3   **Building society finance for houses**

The measure which we shall look at is the 'liquidity ratio' of building societies. This is a measure of the cash and liquid assets held by building societies, available to pay depositors on request, compared with the total amount of money deposited with the societies. The seasonal pattern of this liquidity ratio is given in Figure 13.4. The scale is shown as the deviation in

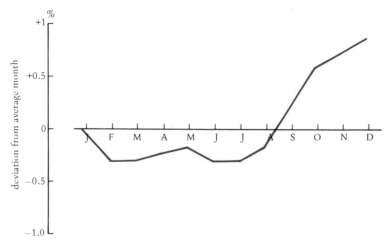

Fig. 13.4 Building societies – liquidity ratio

percentage points; during the period studied, the liquidity ratio averaged rather under 20 per cent, so that a variation of around one percentage point means about 5 per cent in terms of total liquidity.

This pattern reaches a peak in December, when a large net increase in shares and deposits (including interest credited to accounts) coincides with a low level of mortgage advances. It then falls very sharply in January (because of tax payments – although the historical pattern will be somewhat different in the future now that tax payments are made quarterly) and continues to fall as a low intake of funds coincides with an increase in mortgage demand. In fact, building societies are in a particularly unfortunate position, inasmuch as their attraction to investors is seasonally out of step with the interests of borrowers. Fortunately, as we have seen, these variations represent a fairly modest effect of about 5 per cent in the actual amounts of cash readily available to societies.

This is fortunate inasmuch as building societies rightly project an image of safety and security. In the next chapter, we shall look at alternative investments which carry much higher levels of risk.

14   Other personal savings

Stocks and shares are dealt with in the 'business' section of the book. For the private individual, unit trusts have gained in popularity as a means of investing on the stock exchange. Later we shall look at an investment which is regarded as even more speculative, namely premium bonds.

Unit trusts

In the previous chapter, when we looked at building society investment, we looked separately at new deposits and at withdrawals. We shall do the same with unit trusts: in Figure 14.1 are shown the seasonal patterns for buying new units and for selling existing units.

In one sense, these results are very similar to those for building society investments; in another sense they are quite different. They are similar in that the 'buying' and 'selling' patterns are very similar to each other, rather than (as might have been expected) mirror images of each other. On the other hand, the actual monthly pattern differs markedly from the building society patterns. The one month in which there *is* complete similarity on all counts is December: this stands out as a month of low activity, and we shall see exactly the same picture in a minute when we come to premium bonds.

I strongly suspect that the similar patterns for 'buying' and 'selling' are (as with building societies) partly due to the process of switching from one fund to another. The pattern of activity is very similar to that which we shall see in Chapter 17 for share transactions. There is a major peak in the spring, especially in March, and a secondary peak in the autumn. These peaks correspond quite closely to the times when interest rates are at their seasonal

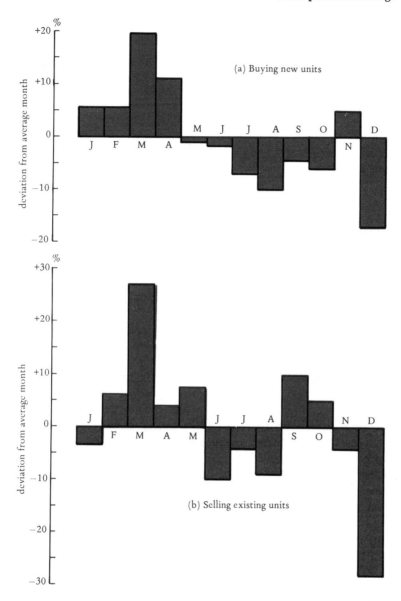

Fig. 14.1 Unit trusts

lows and share prices (as well as the number of share transactions) are
approaching their seasonal highs.

It is understandable that the level of *activity* is low around the Christmas
and summer holiday periods; it is not so immediately obvious why interest

rates should be higher and share prices (and unit trust prices) lower at precisely the same periods. As far as shares and units are concerned, there is a logic: over a long period of time, as wealth accumulates, there is a greater pressure to buy than there is to sell. So, when activity is highest, it will tend to be driven more by buying activity than selling activity. This is illustrated very clearly in the unit trust statistics: on average, the number of units bought is about double the new units sold in any month.

Figure 14.1 refers to the *level of activity* in buying and selling unit trusts. As I have just implied, the *value* of the shares which constitute the units also follows a roughly similar pattern (although the spring peak comes a little later). Much more detail on the seasonal patterns of share prices is given in Chapter 17.

The results show rather clearly the effects of the 'herd' instinct. The increasing interest in buying shares and units in the spring coincides with (and may contribute to) a higher level of prices, so that the majority of purchases are made at the top of the market. When we come to look at share prices, we shall see that there is some advantage in ignoring the 'herd' and buying shares (and unit trusts) when most people are showing rather less interest.

Premium bonds

Premium bonds are often regarded as something of a gamble rather than an investment. This is actually a very misleading way to look at them, as it is only the interest component which is being put at risk; the capital sum remains entirely intact. They are therefore really much *less* risky than unit trusts or shares. However, since they are perceived to be a gamble, they have been chosen as representative of that kind of 'investment'.

The number of existing bonds being sold is, on average, about 57 per cent of the numbers of new bonds being purchased. This is very similar to the rate at which unit trusts are cashed in, but in this case it is quite illogical to sell old bonds to re-invest the proceeds in new bonds. (Nevertheless, I know that some people do do this if 'Ernie' has not chosen any of their existing numbers for a long time). So, again, *transfers* of money out of old bonds and into new ones may partly explain why the patterns shown in Figure 14.2 are not mirror images of each other.

The results of the seasonal analysis were corrected for the different number of days in each month, but not for holidays. We can immediately see in Figure 14.2 the feature mentioned earlier, namely the low activity (both buying and selling) in December.

Also evident – and highlighted by the dotted curve – is the 'M' shape which we first saw with building society data and subsequently with unit trusts. Compared with other examples of the 'M' factor which we shall see, January

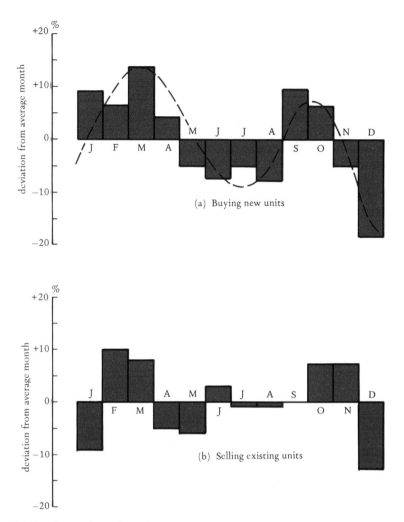

Fig. 14.2 **Premium bonds**

sales of premium bonds are actually somewhat out of line; there is considerably more purchase activity at the start of the New Year than we would expect from the general evidence which we shall find later of a recurrent 'M' factor.

In fact, I shall move straight on now to Part III, to introduce you to some of the many series of business statistics which are characterized by a seasonal 'M' pattern.

Part III
BUSINESS

15 The 'M' factor

The latter chapters of the 'everyday life' section were beginning to overlap with 'business' factors. The housewife's weekly shopping basket is also 'bread and butter' for the businessman. Similarly, the money which is moved into and out of building society accounts plays a very important role in the financial flows in the economy as a whole.

You were introduced, in those latter chapters, to the idea that many series of business and economic data exhibit a seasonal pattern which resembles the letter 'M'. In this chapter, I shall indicate in advance some of the other series of data which exhibit this monthly 'M' factor.

Eight separate examples are presented in Figures 15.1 and 15.2. These cover business confidence indicators, interest rates, ordinary shares and commodity prices.

The interest rate patterns are shown with the scale inverted; in that way, they indicate the patterns appropriate to the *prices* of the stocks which they represent, rather than the interest rates which the stocks carry. Hence, the patterns are more directly comparable with those for share prices.

In this introductory chapter, I should like to draw your attention to both the similarities and the differences between various series.

Probably the most consistent feature of these (and many other) patterns is the strong positive effect in March and April. Sometimes the primary peak of the 'M' also includes February; sometimes it extends to May. But whatever the total span of this primary peak, it *always* includes both March and April.

The primary peak is followed by a trough which typically reaches its lowest point in July. I shall refer to this as the 'secondary trough', as it is almost always less significant than the primary trough which occurs in the late autumn or early winter.

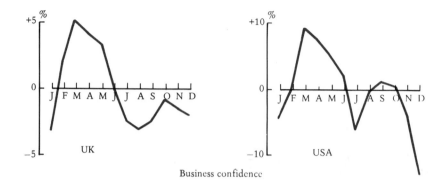

Business confidence

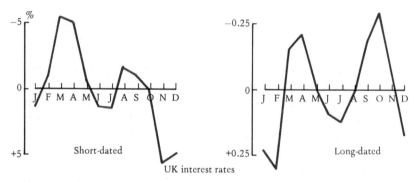

UK interest rates

Fig. 15.1   Examples of the 'M' factor

From July, the pattern rises to a secondary peak which occurs most commonly around September. However, it is neither as consistent in timing nor usually as vigorous as the primary peak. It can occur as early as August or as late as November.

Finally, we come full circle to the primary trough. This is a very pronounced effect, although quite variable in timing. Most typically, the trough occurs in November or December (two or three months after the secondary peak), but occasionally it is delayed until January or February.

I have set out these examples in advance (Figures 15.1 and 15.2), so that you have a general picture in your mind against which to compare each of the individual patterns as we come to them. You will find, in the following chapters, that this general picture of an 'M' pattern is something which is found in very many series, for many different countries and for many different

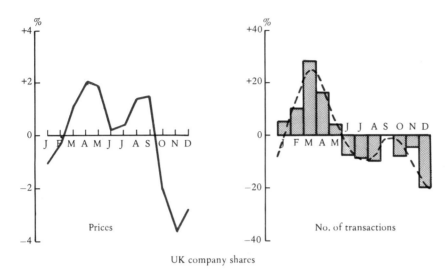

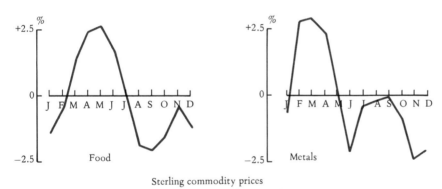

Sterling commodity prices

Fig. 15.2   Further examples of the 'M' factor

time periods. It is so pervasive that it must reflect something quite fundamental about the way in which our developed economies operate.

The first question I am always asked is, what happens on the other side of the world? Are the patterns inverted? Are they six months out of phase? I have to say that the evidence which I can present on these questions is both sparse and confusing. The 'M' pattern itself automatically makes such a comparison difficult, since it breaks down a 12-month pattern roughly into two 6-month patterns. If you shift an 'M' pattern six months to the right, you still end up with an 'M'. Unless there is a clear distinction between the primary and secondary peaks, then it is not possible to say definitely whether a particular pattern (e.g. for Australia) is or is not 6 months out of phase compared to a reference pattern derived from UK data. Generally speaking, the evidence which I shall present indicates that Australia *is* roughly 6 months out of phase.

Within Europe and North America, the general pattern is so common that – well before you reach the end of the book – you may come to be more surprised at the *exceptions* to the pattern than at the 'M' pattern itself! These variations from the normal 'M' pattern are found, for instance, with interest rates and share prices in America. Although I myself don't have any original suggestions to make about these differences, I have quoted in Chapter 23 from some earlier work, published in the US, which throws some light on the question.

This introductory chapter has attempted to set the scene for the seasonal patterns which are presented in the following chapters, for a wide range of factors. The first factor to be presented in detail is business confidence. For various reasons, which I shall explain in the next chapter, it is a particularly useful one to use as a starting point. In addition, this research into the seasonal patterns in business confidence represents what I believe to be an original contribution to economic analysis, which is presented here for the first time.

16 Business confidence

In this chapter, I shall set out the overwhelming evidence of strong seasonality in the optimism and pessimism of businessmen.

Business decisions, particularly on the commitment of money to large-scale capital investments, are very dependent on managers' views about the likely future state of the economy in general and their markets in particular. If there are significant short-term seasonal variations in their perceptions (which there are), then this will introduce some degree of 'irrationality' into those decisions. Moreover, if you know that your suppliers are likely to be pessimistic at certain times, or that your customers are likely to be optimistic at other times, you may be able to use that knowledge to advantage when it comes to timing purchase contracts and price increases respectively.

My own interest in measures of business confidence arises from their value as a measure of the present or future state of the economy, for the purposes of sales forecasting. First, though, I ought to describe the nature of the surveys which are conducted to measure business confidence; they are probably unfamiliar to many readers.

Business opinion surveys

The best-known survey in Britain is the one carried out monthly (and, in more detail, quarterly) by the Confederation of British Industry. The CBI polls a large number of businessmen each month with questions concerning

- the present total order book (and export order book);
- the present level of stocks of finished goods;

- the expected trend in the volume of output, looking four months ahead;
- the expected trend in average prices, also looking four months ahead.

Answers are requested in the form

- above normal/normal/below normal; or
- more than adequate/adequate/less than adequate; or
- up/same/down

as appropriate. The index itself is then calculated as the difference between the 'above normal' and 'below normal' percentage responses (or between 'more' and 'less' or between 'up' and 'down').

Suppose, for instance, that the results of such a survey are:

Question	Your present total order book is . . .	
Responses	Above normal	60%
	Normal	30%
	Below normal	10%

The 'balance of respondents' indicating more favourable business conditions (as measured by order books) would be 60% — 10% = 50%.

I ought to mention that the questionnaires do try to elicit seasonally corrected responses. For instance, the full text of one very important question in the CBI survey is: 'What, *excluding seasonal variations*, is the expected trend over the next four months with regard to the volume of output?' When we come to look at the results (and also the actual variations in output given in Chapter 19) we shall conclude that the responses do *not*, in general, take into account the actual seasonal patterns of output.

Surveys for other countries

The value of this kind of survey has been recognized for a long time in Europe, and much greater use is made of them on the Continent. I have analysed data for all of the larger countries of the EEC.

The precise form of the questions may vary slightly from country to country, but not sufficiently to affect inter-country comparisons. The particular question which I have found to be most useful is the one concerning 'production (or output) expectations'. *All* of the national surveys contain a similar question on this subject.

In the United States less use is made of such surveys, although an excellent one is carried out monthly by their National Association of Purchasing

Management (NAPM). We shall look at the results of that survey later.

There is a very good review of the various national surveys in Chapter 5 of *Monitoring Growth Cycles in Market Oriented Countries*, by Philip A. Klein and Geoffrey H. Moore, published in 1985 by the National Bureau of Economic Research. The odd thing about an otherwise comprehensive review is that they completely ignore their own country's NAPM survey, which is perhaps indicative of the relatively low interest generally shown in the United States in such measures of economic activity.

Why study business opinion?

It may seem strange to start a review of seasonal factors in business by looking at measures of business opinion. There are several good reasons for doing so, which I should like to explain.

The first reason is a very personal one. My interest in the whole subject of seasonality was kindled by the detection of strong seasonal patterns in surveys of business conditions. This chapter is the first time I have presented a summary of the results of extensive personal research into the subject.

Secondly, these surveys are gaining in credibility and popularity as ways of monitoring and projecting changes in the state of the economy.

A particular advantage of these surveys for the forecaster is that they are very up to date: the results are published within days of the surveys being carried out. All economists are familiar with a problem associated with the use of many official statistics: by the time the figures are published, sometimes several months in arrears, it is often too late to make much use of them.

The situation with 'conventional' statistics is often even worse than that. Subsequent revisions to the data can completely alter the original picture. We have seen a classic example of this in recent years with the quarterly figures for the Gross National Product of the USA, which is a very important lead indicator of subsequent events in other parts of the world. Several times recently, the initial data (especially the 'flash' estimates) have been radically changed by later adjustments. Business surveys, on the other hand, are both timely and free from later modification.

As to seasonality, they are also very sensitive. This may be surprising, in view of the way the questions are phrased. However, I have found in practice that the seasonal patterns which they exhibit are often much more significant, statistically, than similar patterns which occur in other series such as interest rates.

There is one common criticism of these surveys which, in fact, I believe to be entirely misplaced. The criticism is often made that the surveys elicit highly subjective responses; also, that the respondents don't really treat the questions all that seriously when filling in the questionnaires. This means (rightly) that the results have no absolute meaning. However, so long as the questions and the sample of respondents are consistent from one monthly survey to another, the lack of any precise meaning really doesn't matter; it is a valid method of tracking *changes* in confidence. The fact that the actual numbers don't mean anything precise does not alter the fact that the general shape of the results, when graphed over a period of time, *does* give a very good impression of the way in which business confidence and business conditions are fluctuating up and down. Moreover − and this is the key point − these changes do reflect (or, in some cases, lead) the general ups and downs in the demand for many specific products.

I actually believe that the casual manner in which the forms are completed (and I've filled in a few myself over the years!) is actually a good thing. If the respondents sat down to think through the questions in any depth, they would start to think of all kinds of reasons why their off-the-cuff reactions might not be valid. The very spontaneity of the responses means that they capture some kind of mentally weighted average of all of the factors which are influencing their business at that time.

So, to summarize, I find these surveys to be timely, stable, sensitive . . . and, what is more to the point, useful!

The importance of seasonal adjustment

Since these surveys are so useful, and since the seasonal effects are so large, I do think that it is important that the results should be published in a seasonally-adjusted form. In the United States, the NAPM 'composite index' is, in fact, corrected in this way. In the UK, the survey results are not seasonally corrected; as a result, the 'raw' data will tend to give an over-optimistic view of the underlying situation in the spring and an over-pessimistic view in the autumn.

Results for the UK

By way of introduction, Figure 16.1 presents the seasonal pattern for the UK surveys of 'production expectations'. The CBI survey data cover a slightly longer period than the EEC data which I have used. The two patterns are quite similar and are both examples of the 'M' factor. It is perhaps interesting to see the two in one diagram, to illustrate the kind of differences which you might expect by analysing different time periods.

It is immediately obvious that the survey responses do *not* include any accurate mental correction for seasonal factors; if they did accurately reflect such factors, then there would be no detectable seasonal pattern at all in the responses.

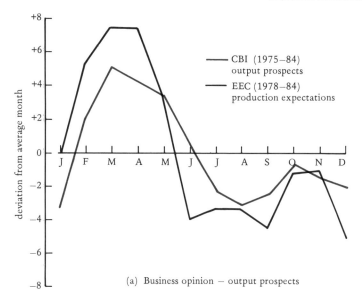

(a) Business opinion – output prospects

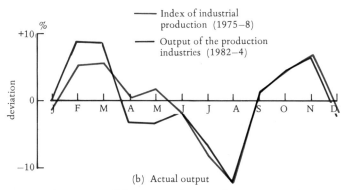

(b) Actual output

Fig. 16.1   Business confidence and actual output

Also in Figure 16.1 is the seasonal pattern of actual output, of which more will be said in Chapter 19. With the exception of the high level of business confidence in April, the two charts show patterns which are rather similar in their general shape. It would be reasonable to infer, from this, that business opinion of future prospects four months hence bears a much closer resemblance to the *current* situation than it does to the *future* situation.

This is not to say that business opinion is dictated *solely* by the current level of output. Far from it. We shall see later that there are several other factors which produce similar patterns and which might be contributory factors; the level of interest rates, for instance, is likely to be an important determinant of business optimism.

Turning to Figure 16.2, you can see how the seasonal pattern can vary from one year to another. This figure also shows how the index faithfully reflects the general state of the economy: the 1980/81 recession stands out very clearly. In this diagram, I have broken into the 12-month moving average for two years, 1977 and 1979, to show the actual monthly data for those years. You can compare the actual data for each year with the average seasonal pattern shown in red.

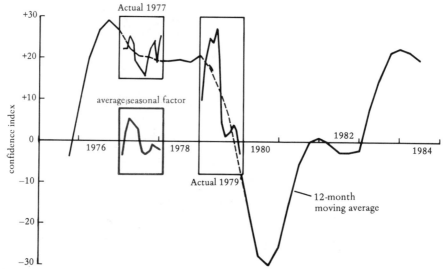

Fig. 16.2   CBI survey – output prospects

You might have guessed that, when the general level of business confidence is falling very rapidly (as it was in 1979 at the time of the second oil crisis), the seasonal variations would have been completely lost in the general collapse of confidence. This is clearly not the case: the seasonal pattern is actually *more* pronounced when the underlying trend is changing very rapidly. You will also see that the seasonal effect accounts for a substantial part of the total variation in the survey data: it is *not* just a minor variation superimposed on a strong trend.

Figure 16.3 shows the seasonal patterns for three other CBI series, namely prices, total orders and export orders. These are included for two reasons: first, the patterns are different from the output series; secondly, there is something peculiar about the results. You may recall that I mentioned that the CBI carry out a more detailed survey every three months–January, April,

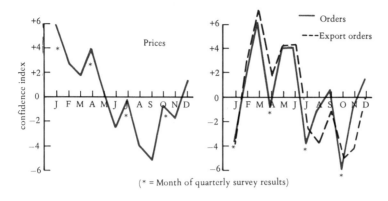

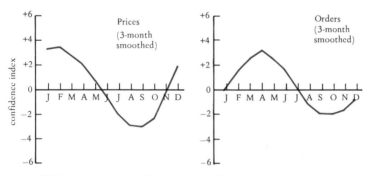

Fig. 16.3   CBI survey – prices and orders

July and October to be precise. It is clear that the data for prices and orders are really made up from two different series: (a) the months in which a more detailed survey is carried out; and (b) the intervening months, when a simpler questionnaire is used. It may well be that two different groups of people tend to answer the two different questionnaires. Whatever the reason, there is clear evidence of a quarterly pattern superimposed on the underlying monthly pattern.

The solution to this kind of problem is to smooth the data by taking 3-month moving averages. This eliminates the effect of the quarterly distortions, but it also masks some of the fine detail of the seasonal pattern.

With that proviso, we can use the 3-month averages to see more clearly the general patterns. Optimism on future price increases rises as the New Year approaches, and continues into the spring. The actual level of order books follows a similar pattern two months later. These patterns are quite unusual, as far as these surveys are concerned, in *not* conforming to an 'M' shape.

Results for Europe

As I mentioned earlier, the best series to work with for the purposes of forecasting are those measuring 'production expectations'. Figures 16.4 and 16.5 show these patterns plotted for seven separate European countries (including the UK) and also for the EEC in total.

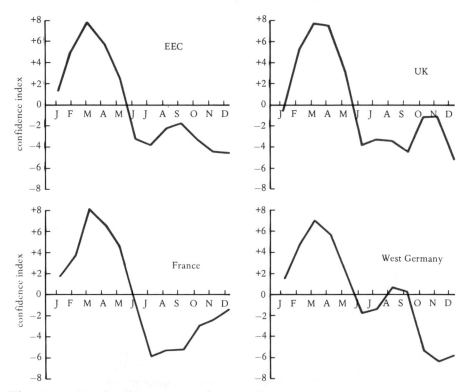

Fig. 16.4   Production expectations – Europe

Of the seven separate country charts, six show clear 'M' patterns; the odd one out is France, for which the secondary peak is missing.

No doubt you will also notice that Ireland is also somewhat out of line with other countries! Its 'M' pattern has a particularly sharp fall in the middle of the year, but also a very strong secondary peak; it is also the only country which has a relatively weak primary peak in the spring. Otherwise, the shape of the primary peak is remarkably similar for all of the individual countries.

For most countries, the secondary peak is around September. The UK is rather different in this respect, as this peak arrives two months later than for other countries.

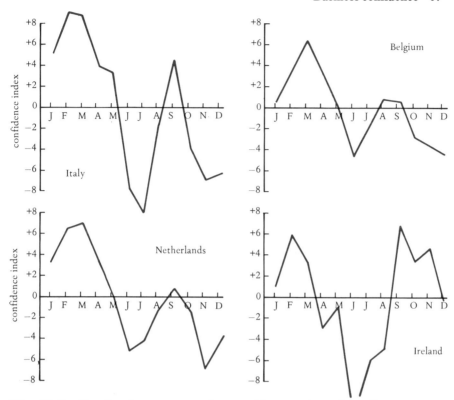

Fig. 16.5   Production expectations – Europe (continued)

The most pronounced seasonal effect shown in these diagrams is for Italy. We shall see later, in Chapter 17, that this pattern is almost exactly reproduced in the seasonal variations in Italian stock market prices.

The subsequent graphs for Europe are all based on aggregate data for the whole of the EEC. Figure 16.6 shows the patterns for order books and for stocks of finished products. You can see how the order books pattern, in this case, does have a secondary peak – something which was lost in the UK data by the process of taking a 3-month moving average. However, this secondary peak – in both orders and stocks – is rather weak. Also, the seasonal factors for the whole year are much less pronounced than they are with the production expectation series (note the different scales).

The 'stock levels' results are plotted with the scale upside down. The reason for this is that high stocks are a *negative* factor – at least, that is how they are judged by most businessmen; conversely, one sign of buoyant business conditions is a low level of stocks.

The European data are reported, not only by country, but also by industrial category. I thought that seasonal changes might start with companies closer to

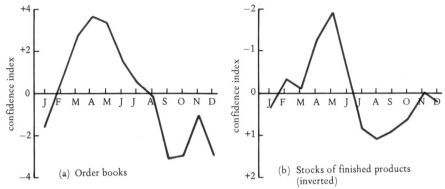

Fig. 16.6   EEC surveys – orders and stocks

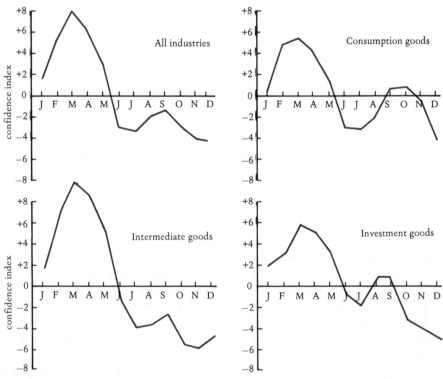

Fig. 16.7   Production expectations – European industry sectors

the final customer, then gradually work their way back – with appropriate time delays – via intermediate goods producers to those companies supplying capital goods. In fact, there is no evidence of any such effect: the patterns given in Figure 16.7 are all very similar, with the one exception that the primary peak is particularly strong and the secondary peak very weak for the suppliers of intermediate goods. All of the patterns exhibit the 'M' factor to a greater or lesser extent.

Results for the United States

The US National Association of Purchasing Management publish the results of several monthly series, four of which are illustrated in Figure 16.8. One series which is omitted is the so-called 'composite index', the only one for which the results are published in a seasonally adjusted form. I did carry out a seasonal analysis on this index and, indeed, I could not detect any significant residual seasonal pattern; in other words, the published figures *do* adequately correct for seasonality.

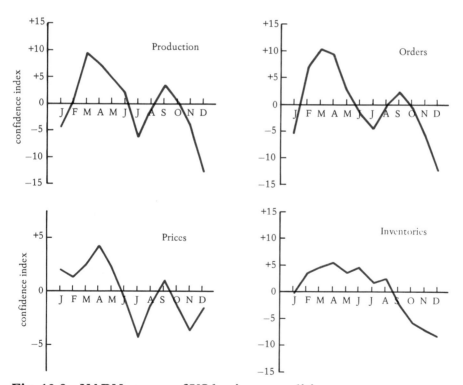

Fig. 16.8   NAPM survey of US business conditions

The presence of seasonality in the individual components is very clear from Figure 16.8. In fact, the month-to-month variations are really very large indeed. For instance, the variation in the seasonal factors for the 'production' series covers a range of about 20 percentage points; the *total* variability of the series is such that, in a typical year, the values cover a range of perhaps 40 percentage points. Hence, the seasonal effect represents as much as half of the total spread of results which might occur in a year.

The UK and European surveys specifically ask respondents to comment on their views of production prospects a few months hence. The US survey, on the other hand, asks how *current* production levels differ from those one month earlier. Thus, the latter is quite explicitly intended to measure current business conditions. The fact that the patterns for the USA and for Europe are nevertheless so similar is simply a further illustration of the fact that opinions about the future usually reflect conditions in the present.

The US seasonal patterns for both production and orders clearly reproduce an 'M' shape in the annual pattern of output. The 'prices' series differs slightly, but not unexpectedly, inasmuch as it reflects a common emphasis on December/January as a time for price increases.

You will remember that, when we looked at the European survey results, the 'finished stock' series were plotted with the scales inverted. To have done the same with the US 'inventories' series would have led to a pattern which would have been completely out of line with its companion series. You may think that I have been rather arbitrary in the way in which I have treated these two series so as to conform with the patterns found for the other factors. In fact, this is not so. The US 'inventories' series refers to inventories of *purchased* materials rather than of finished products. You can see, in Figure 16.9, the relationships between, on the one hand, the finished goods and inventory series and, on the other hand, the corresponding production series.

In the UK, high confidence (as expressed via the production series) is associated with finished stocks which are regarded as *less* than average. Meanwhile, in the US, a high rating for production is directly associated with a *high* rating on inventories of purchased materials. Thus, it is correct to invert the UK 'stocks' series but not the US 'inventories' series.

It is worth looking more closely at the production series for the two countries, shown in Figure 16.9. You will see that changes in direction in the US series typically occur some 6 months in advance of the turning points in the UK one. Thus, it looks as if we have found, in the US production series, a 'lead indicator' of future business conditions in Britain.

(If you decide to use the NAPM data as a lead indicator in this way, remember to adjust the data seasonally before you use them for forecasting! The best approach in practice is to do what I have done in Figure 16.9, namely to plot 12-month moving averages).

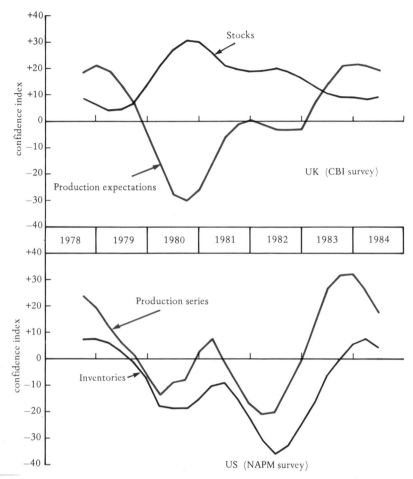

**Fig. 16.9   Relationships between stocks/inventory series for
different periods**

Historical evidence from the US

We are fortunate in having NAPM survey data going back for many years.
The results for four separate periods, going back to 1948, are shown in Figure
16.10.

Since 1956 the seasonal pattern has been quite remarkably consistent. It was
different prior to 1956, but not all that much. In fact, the only real difference
was that the economy was then rather less buoyant in the period February to
June.

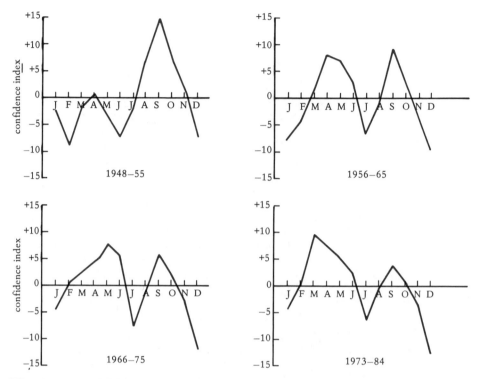

Fig. 16.10   NAPM production series for different periods

Results for other countries

Both Australia and Japan have their own surveys of business conditions; unfortunately, they are published only at quarterly intervals. Also, I do not know whether or not the results are reported quickly after the surveys are conducted. All of this makes positive comparisons with our own series very difficult. All I have been able to do is to indicate that the results for Australia are at least consistent with what you might expect for the other side of the world.

In saying that, I am assuming that you would expect Australia to be about 6 months out of phase with Britain. In fact, the results for the two countries are quite similar if the Australian results are plotted 7 months earlier (which is the same as 5 months later) than the UK results. In other words, January in the UK seems to be equivalent to June in Australia. The results are shown in Figure 16.11. This comparison is by no means exact, but is probably at least as good as one might reasonably expect.

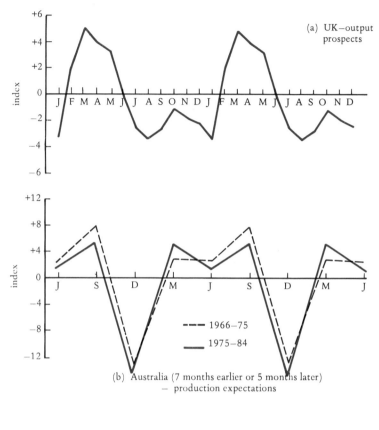

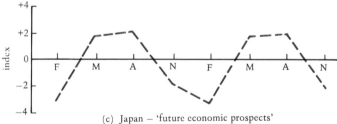

Fig. 16.11   Comparison with Pacific area countries

Figure 16.11(b) also shows that the seasonal pattern of business confidence in Australia seems to be a very consistent phenomenon: the patterns for two different time periods are almost exactly the same.

The Australian results are much as expected, whereas the Japanese ones are rather inscrutable. In the case of Japan, there is no logical reason to expect it to differ from other countries in the northern hemisphere. However, differ it does. Japanese businessmen are significantly more confident in the summer than in the winter. (I'm sure that there must be some way of interpreting this observation which would help us to compete more effectively against them!)

Concluding remarks

I have spent a considerable time researching these business conditions surveys, and reporting them here, because I believe that they are much more useful tools of economic analysis than they are usually given credit for.

An excellent review of these surveys is given in the book which I referred to earlier by Philip Klein and Geoffrey Moore. They compare, in considerable detail, the relationships between the qualitative survey results and actual turning points in the real economy. One conclusion is that survey results give fewer 'false signals':

> One of the principal strengths of the survey replies is their greater smoothness. This characteristic, together with the tendency of survey results to be available before the quantitative equivalents, contributes one of the major reasons for considering qualitative indicators along with quantitative indicators in developing indicators for forecasting.

But do remember that the monthly data are very strongly influenced by seasonal factors.

One value of these surveys, for forecasting purposes, is that they give one of the best up-to-date measures of what is actually happening *today*. Several of the questions are actually supposed to elicit opinion on *future* conditions. In practice, my own experience is exactly in line with a comment made by Klein and Moore, in respect of the German data which they analysed:

> The evidence suggests that entrepreneurs expect production levels to be in line with those they are currently experiencing.

Moreover, what Klein and Moore found for Germany is, I'm sure, equally true for other countries, and also for series other than production prospects. (We shall see the same kind of effect when we come to the monthly variations in exchange rates.) This in no way diminishes the value of the surveys in economic analysis. For instance, we saw earlier how survey data for the US could be used as a lead indicator of conditions in Britain.

Having looked at the way businessmen view the world outside, I would like now to look at how the world views those businessmen and their companies.

TECHNICAL NOTE (A)

Test for statistical significance

The moving average process gives us a graph of the longer-term trends and cycles. We then take the difference between each individual data point and its moving average to estimate the seasonal effect for that month. The difference which we calculate for, say, January will not be the same for each year; we get a spread of differences because of the impact of all kinds of random, unpredictable effects. Sometimes the differences for January might be randomly spread around zero, i.e. there might be roughly as many January values above their moving average as there are below their moving average. In that case, the average of the January deviations won't necessarily be exactly zero, but it won't be all that different from zero. There is a straightforward analysis to test whether a set of seasonal factors are sufficiently different from zero to be regarded as statistically significant. The method compares the variation *between* the average values for each month with the random variation which is found *within* each month. If the ratio of the two is greater than a tabulated figure, then we can reasonably assume that the difference between the months is a significant one, which would be unlikely to have arisen by chance.

The result of applying this analysis to the CBI 'output expectations' series was as follows:

Source of variation	Sum of squares	Degrees of freedom	Variance
Between months	884.7	11	80.4
Within months	2813.0	96	29.3
Total	3697.7	107	34.6

The ratio of the 'between months' variance to the 'within months' variance is 2.74. There is less than 1 chance in 100 that a ratio as high as this could be a chance occurrence. The closer the ratio is to 1, the more likely it is that the month-to-month differences are purely random.

If all of this sounds a little confusing, don't worry. The computer program which is described at the end of the book will carry out this calculation automatically, and let you know whether the seasonal factors calculated for your own data are statistically significant or not.

TECHNICAL NOTE (B)

The CBI itself has recently started to look at the possibility that its survey results exhibit significant seasonal effects. Two recent and relevant articles are: 'How the CBI interprets the Industrial Trends Survey', by D. F. McWilliams, in *Twenty-five years of 'ups' and 'downs'*, published by the CBI in October 1983; and 'Seasonality and CBI Industrial Trends Data: An Exploratory Note', by G. N. Robinson, in *Economic Situation Report*, published by the CBI in October 1985.

In the first of these two articles, McWilliams says:

> . . . the results of the surveys have shown a distinctly seasonal pattern since 1972. . . . However, it might be argued that over this period economic developments themselves have had an unusual seasonal pattern. For example, the ending of major strikes in the Springs of 1974, 1979 and 1980 might account for some of the buoyancy of the April results. The issue of whether the Industrial Trends Survey results have seasonal biases is therefore not yet finally resolved.

This 'open' verdict reflects a conclusion reached much earlier by D. J. Reid (in *Applied Economics*, vol. 1, 1969). At that time he had only a very short series of data to work on, and concluded:

> There seems to be some evidence that the expectations data are not entirely free of seasonality.

I hope that my own analysis leaves no doubt about the seasonal characteristics of the results: it's not just that the seasonal effects are statistically significant in their own right, but also that they are so similar to many other seasonal patterns.

The article by Robinson was based on the calculation of auto-correlation functions and power spectra (techniques which were mentioned briefly in Chapter 3). He actually concluded that there is little evidence of strong seasonal frequencies in the main CBI series. I suspect that this is because the series are dominated by strong, longer-term cycles of varying periods and that these effects (which are removed in the moving average process) confuse the results.

Both papers refer to the differences and lack of comparability between the monthly and quarterly surveys.

17 Stock markets

For a change, we shall start with data for the United States. The reason for this is that it offers the advantage of being able to compare the results with previously published work; we shall then move on to the UK, Europe and other countries.

North American stock markets

The analysis for the USA was based on the value of the Dow Jones industrial index at the end of each month. The result was a great disappointment—an entirely random pattern; no pattern at all, in fact. (Don't now immediately turn to the next chapter: the results for the UK are much more interesting!)

This result does differ slightly from some work published in America. A paper entitled 'Year-End Tax-Induced Sales and Stock Market Seasonality' by Dan Givoly and Arie Ovadin was published in the *Journal of Finance*, vol. 38, no. 1, in 1983. It was based on stock market prices covering the whole of the period 1945–79, and represents perhaps the best detailed study of stock market seasonality in the United States. It is also particularly useful for anyone interested in studying this stock market in detail, as it provides a list of other relevant publications. Only the last four years of their study overlap with the 1976–84 period which I have used, so that we are not really comparing like with like.

They also found that in general there was no significant seasonal pattern – but with one exception. Share prices *did* tend to rise consistently in January; the seasonal effect represented about a 4 per cent rise in that month. They also reported that the effect was particularly pronounced for the shares of small firms; these are not included in the Dow Jones Industrial Average, which probably explains part, at least, of the difference between their conclusions and mine.

January has a special place in the mythology of Wall Street. There is a saying that, if prices rise in January (some say in the first few days of January), then they will end the whole year higher than where they started. There is often more than a grain of truth in these 'old brokers' tales', as we shall see when we come to look at UK data. It may therefore be the case that shares generally *did* rise in January; since shares also tend to rise more often than they fall when measured over a whole year, it would then follow naturally that a correlation could well be discovered between a January rise and a yearly rise.

Staying in North America for a minute, the Toronto Stock Exchange Corporate Index does show some seasonality, as shown in Figure 17.1. The pattern for the first half-year is not statistically significant and should be ignored; however, the rise from October to December is large enough (and consistent enough) to be unlikely to be a chance occurrence. In fact, prices in December exceeded their 12-month moving average in every year except one. This second half-year has a very similar pattern to the UK (Figure 17.2), albeit with a much more vigorous recovery from the October low. Completely missing, though, is the strong performance in March/April which is a characteristic of so many series of data.

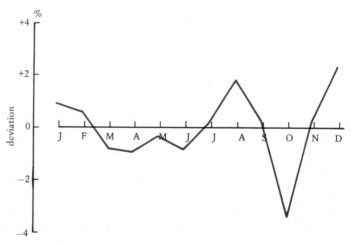

Fig. 17.1   Canadian share prices

The UK stock market

The UK pattern in Figure 17.2 is calculated from the Financial Times Actuaries All-Share Index at the end of each month. We were talking earlier about stock market adages; a popular one in Britain is 'sell in May and go away'. The calculated seasonal pattern shows that early May is, indeed, the time to sell shares if you have to; prices at the end of April tend to be higher than at the end of May, by about 4 per cent. (There is no popular adage which indicates when to *buy* shares. In the light of the results presented here, perhaps it should be, 'remember, remember to buy in November'.)

In recent years, between the end of April and the end of October, there has been a purely seasonal decline of around 8 per cent on average. This has to be set against the fact that, over the period 1976–84, the UK stock market was actually going up by around 15 per cent pa, which means that share prices didn't usually fall from May to October, they just didn't rise. Looked at the other way round, there was only one year in which a good rise was *not* seen from the end of October to the end of the following April.

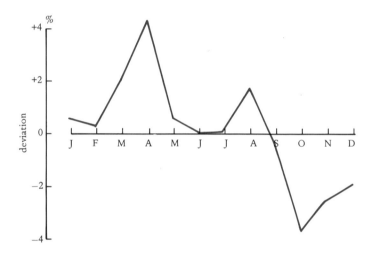

Fig. 17.2   UK share prices (end of month)

Figure 17.2 is based on *month-end* data, so as to be consistent with data used for other countries. On the other hand, share prices published by the Central Statistical Office are monthly *averages*. These average prices are also given for various subcategories of shares; the seasonal analysis of those series is summarized in Figure 17.3. If you start with Figure 17.3a, the 'all shares' index, you will notice minor differences compared with Figure 17.2: the primary peak has been flattened out somewhat, and the whole graph has (as you would expect) been displaced to the right by about half a month. For instance, the deviation for May based on *average* monthly data (about +2 per

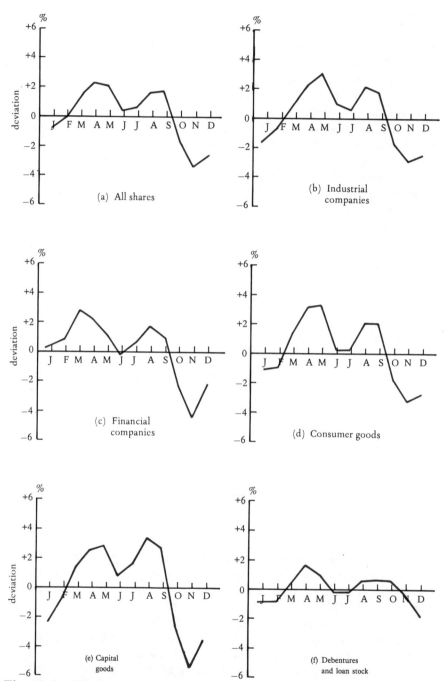

Fig. 17.3   UK share prices by industry sector (monthly averages)

cent) is roughly the average of the deviations for end-April and end-May shown in Figure 17.2.

The 'M' factor is strongly in evidence, whether month-end or monthly average data are studied. What is more, there is remarkably little difference between the five patterns for the various categories of ordinary shares shown in Figure 17.3; indeed, they are virtually identical. One subtle difference is that the month-to-month variations in the capital goods sector are about half as much again as the corresponding variations in the other sectors. Capital goods companies are generally the ones which are most sensitive to changes in interest rates; and we shall not be surprised later on if we find that the seasonal pattern in interest rates is very similar to that in share prices.

In fact, we can already anticipate that fact from Figure 17.3f. The prices of debentures and loan stocks are inevitably tied directly to the prices of other fixed-interest bearing stocks (and, therefore, inversely related to the level of long-term interest rates). The patterns for the other categories of shares shown in Figure 17.3 are very similar to the pattern of *short*-term, rather than long-term, interest rates.

It's not only the *prices* of shares which follow the 'M' pattern; a similar picture is found when analysing the *number* of share transactions each month. The results of that analysis are shown in Figure 17.4. Monthly totals were corrected for the number of days in each month, but not for public holidays. This partly explains the only difference between Figures 17.3 and 17.4, namely the low level of transactions in December.

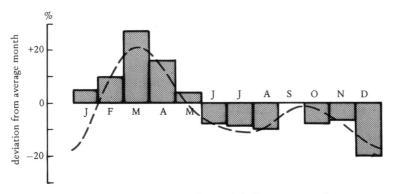

Fig. 17.4   Ordinary shares – number of daily transactions

With the exception of December, we have a situation which is now starting to become familiar: seasonal patterns in both activity and optimism going hand in hand, reaching a peak around March/April, with a secondary peak in the autumn.

Comparison between London and Wall Street

One adage which does not stand up to analysis is the idea that 'when Wall Street coughs, London sneezes'. There was certainly no similarity between the two when we looked at the seasonal patterns. I thought that it might, therefore, be interesting to see if the longer-term trends (as shown by the 12-month moving averages) were similar. You can see from Figure 17.5 that, during recent years, it would be difficult to conclude that there was a relationship between the two graphs. Some of the turning points in the curves are roughly coincident, but others certainly are not.

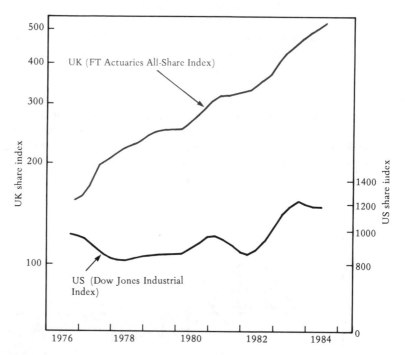

Fig. 17.5   Comparison between share price trends in the UK and the US

Earlier years

It's always interesting to see whether the kind of seasonal patterns which exist today have been present in earlier years. For UK share prices, Figure 17.6 compares two periods: (a) 1976–84 and (b) 1964–72. Initially, the patterns seem rather different. The main difference is the positive deviation which

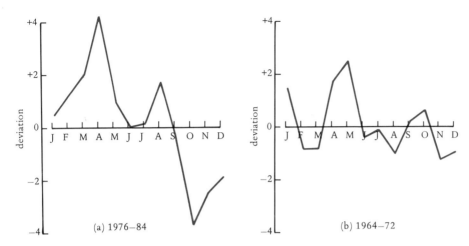

Fig. 17.6   **UK share prices for two time periods**

occurred in January in the earlier period; also, the secondary peak came a little later in the year in those days.

Looking more closely at the computer print-out for the earlier period, it is clear that the January anomaly was due to just two years (1969 and 1970), in which share prices were firm at the beginning of the year. Otherwise, the patterns for the two different periods would actually have been very similar indeed.

European stock markets

Neither France nor Germany produced any strong evidence of seasonality in share prices. In each case, there was one part of the year which showed up something which was just about significant, namely:

Germany—high at the end of April
France—low in June and July

Both of these features are, of course, in line with the UK market at those times of the year.

The one other European country which I analysed was Italy, and share prices there do show a significant seasonal pattern over the whole year. Milan (Figure 17.7) is very much in line with the London stock exchange, except that it does not start to pick up until January. (You will recall that UK share prices were tending to move up in December.)

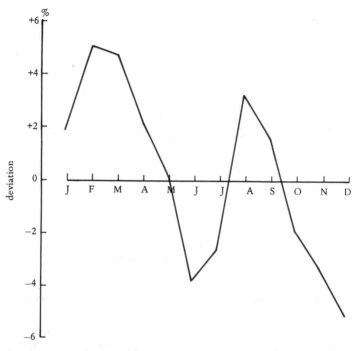

Fig. 17.7   Share prices – Italy

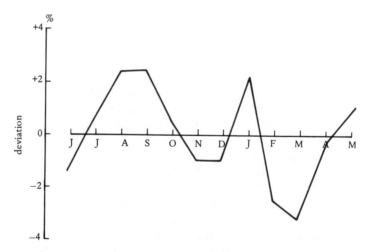

Fig. 17.8   Share prices – Australia

The Pacific area

We found in Chapter 16 that the business confidence pattern in Australia was roughly similar to that in Britain, but displaced by about 6 months. To be more precise, it was necessary to shift the time scale either 7 months backwards or 5 months forwards (which amounts to the same thing). In other words, we plotted the June figure for Australia in line with the January figure for the UK. We can do the same thing with share prices. In this case, we have the advantage of having monthly—rather than just quarterly—data to work on. I am sure that you will find the results of doing this just as interesting as I did. They are given in Figure 17.8.

It is tempting to read perhaps too much into this graph, given the wide degree of error associated with any single point. With that caveat, what seems to be happening is this: (a) the Australian stock exchange has a seasonal pattern very similar to that in Europe (i.e. it peaks in the Australian spring just as Europe peaks in the European spring); (b) superimposed on this pattern is some spin-off from the buoyancy which exists in the northern hemisphere in April and May.

Another southern hemisphere stock exchange is Johannesburg. The South African economy is profoundly influenced by the ups and downs of the gold price; hence this stock market is considered along with gold in Chapter 25. The results are just as intriguing as those for Australia.

We travel back to the northern hemisphere for the last stages of our journey around the world's stock markets. The 'diary' of this part of our journey is reproduced in Figure 17.9.

The first stop-over is Tokyo. Shares in Japan show the familiar strength in spring and weakness towards the end of the year; however, the magnitude of these effects is rather small.

There is nothing stable and steady about the other stock markets in the Far East. Hong Kong has long been regarded as the place for investors seeking high risks and high rewards. You would think, from Figure 17.9b, that the seasonal variations for Hong Kong would be much more statistically significant than those for Japan. Actually, this is not the case. The general level of variability in Hong Kong is such that the pattern which I have reproduced is subject to a great deal of statistical uncertainty.

The same is true of Singapore and Malaysia. These are shown separately, although in fact they are closely linked: a substantial proportion of shares are traded on both exchanges. (It would, therefore, have come as a shock if the seasonal patterns had been different from each other!) Moreover, these markets are very narrow ones, with a rather limited number of shares being traded.

All one can say about these more volatile exchanges is that they seem to lead a life of their own!

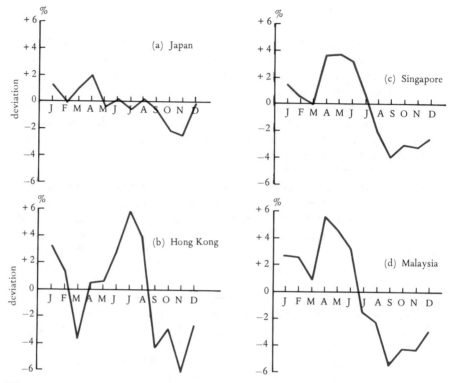

Fig. 17.9   Pacific area stock markets

Summary

What we have seen on our travels is a strong (and familiar) seasonal pattern in the UK and in Italy; much weaker patterns in other European countries and Japan; a mixed pattern in Australia, quite different patterns in the other Far East countries, and no pattern at all in the United States. At least our journey has not been short of variety!

The stock market is just one of the means by which companies raise money. In the next chapter we shall turn to some of the other methods, and look also at company start-ups and failures.

18 Company start-ups and new capital

Buying shares can be the result of quite spontaneous decisions. The euphoria which builds up in the spring can very quickly be translated into action, just by placing an order with a broker or by a visit to the bank.

If a company decides to raise money to finance expansion, this is hardly a spur-of-the-moment decision. The seasonal patterns are therefore likely to reflect a more considered decision-making process. The resulting patterns are illustrated in Figure 18.1.

New equity issues—whether completely new issues of ordinary shares or 'rights' issues to existing shareholders—are much more popular around mid-year than at any other time. (Note the magnitude of the seasonal effects.) The peak comes some two months later than the primary peak in stock markets prices. In fact, the peak coincides with the secondary *trough* in share prices. Although the timing of these new issues could be worse (they could be timed for the last quarter), it is by no means the best time to go to the market.

It often happens, in cases like this, that it is not really possible to disentangle cause and effect. By that, I mean that either or both of the following may contribute to the seasonal patterns which we have observed in the various series:

(a) new issue activity could be a delayed *effect* of the normal spring-time 'boom' (and the rising stock market); or
(b) the seasonally high issue of new shares in mid-year may actually be one *cause* of the fall in share prices at that time.

Issues of new loan capital—Figure 18.1c—follow the stock market trends more closely: the pattern is displaced just one month to the right in

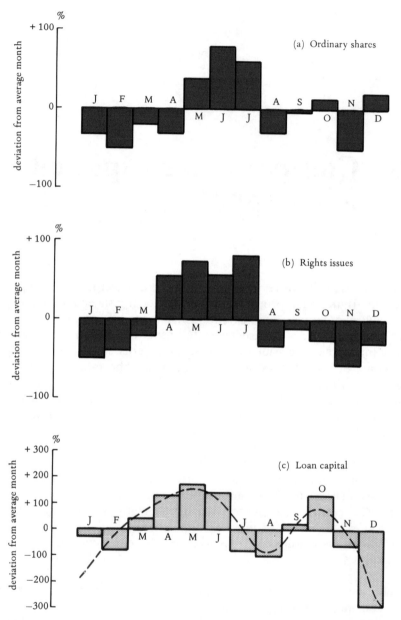

Fig. 18.1   Raising company finance (new issues less redemptions)

comparison with the share price patterns given in Figure 17.3. In the case of loan capital, it might be more relevant to compare Figure 18.1c with the seasonal patterns of interest rates (which we shall see in Chapter 22). In fact, the result is exactly the same: the pattern for the net new issues of loan capital lags behind the interest rate pattern by one month. Apart from this short lag, the *shape* of the patterns (of net new issues and interest rates) is remarkably similar; the *magnitude* of the effects is startlingly different. With interest rates, the maximum seasonal variation from peak to trough is about 10 per cent of the average yearly value; the month-to-month variation in net new issues is many times greater than this.

You will have noticed that I keep referring to 'net' new issues: in other words, the difference between actual new issues and the redemption (repayment) of loan stocks or shares. Since most loan capital has a finite, defined life to maturity, the 'net' figures for loan capital in particular include the effects of substantial redemptions. This explains, incidentally, why the figure for December can be so far below − 100 per cent. A deviation of exactly − 100 per cent below the monthly average would mean an actual level of zero for that month. In the case of loan capital, the December figure is not just zero but is, in fact, *negative*–and by a considerable amount. It is the month in which redemptions of existing loan capital reach a peak.

What we are seeing, in summary, is this. The relatively small (but significant) monthly variations in share prices and interest rates reflect a quite large monthly variation in the way in which business conditions are perceived. We saw this earlier, when we analysed the data from business conditions surveys. These seasonal effects in attitudes are further amplified into even more substantial variations in specific business decisions. If most businessmen (and their financial advisors) consider that a certain time of the year is the best period to go to the market, then even if they all think so by only a small margin, the result is to induce a huge seasonal effect in the end result of their individual deliberations.

There is a new mathematical theory which shows how relatively small changes (e.g. in opinions) can have dramatic effects on the outcome of consequent decisions. It is appropriately called 'catastrophe theory'. I don't know whether the phenomenon which I have described above is, indeed, a practical example of catastrophe theory at work: I should be very interested to know.

For the more unfortunate companies, the ultimate catastrophe is to go into liquidation. The seasonal patterns of both new registrations and liquidations are given in Figure 18.2. These patterns are quite different from those which we have just been studying. This is not surprising. Buying of shares can be virtually spontaneous; raising new money for expansion takes rather more consideration; starting new companies (or

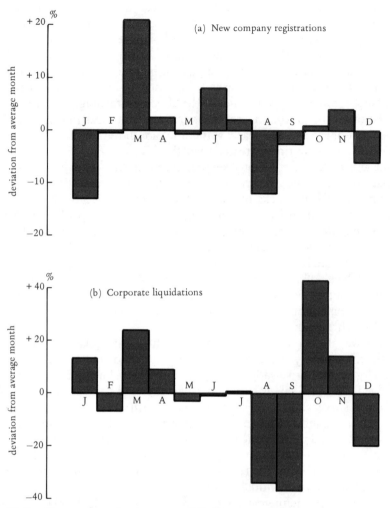

Fig. 18.2   Company start-ups and failures

closing existing ones) is a much longer-term decision altogether; it will be much less susceptible to the monthly variations in business attitudes.

The most consistent features of these charts are the low levels of activity in the holiday months of August and December, and the greater activity in March. Otherwise, it is difficult to draw any meaningful conclusions from the patterns.

In the process of studying these factors, I also looked at the seasonal (quarterly) variation in acquisitions and mergers. Although there has been a slight tendency for such activity to be rather higher in the first and fourth quarters of the year, the differences were not significant.

Having seen the patterns of company start-ups, and the means by which they raise extra finance for expansion, we shall turn next to the output from our companies.

19   Output

The economy as a whole

Data for the 'Gross National Product' (GNP) are published on a quarterly basis. Actually, calculating the figures is not exactly a straightforward task. There are, in fact, three different measures, of which we shall look at two, namely those based on aggregating (a) expenditure and (b) incomes. Since income and expenditure are not necessarily exactly in phase, there are some differences between the two estimates of GNP.

This explains why the seasonal patterns shown in Figure 19.1 are different. The differences between the two measures are particularly pronounced in the second quarter.

Nevertheless, there are some clear and consistent features. Total GNP in the second quarter – the time of year when business confidence and financial

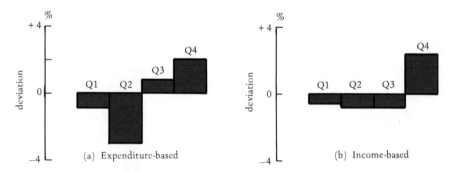

Fig. 19.1   Gross National Product

activity are in full swing − is actually below average. On the other hand, the exact opposite happens in the final quarter: confidence and financial activity are both at low levels, but total economic activity is high.

In fact, the 'M' shaped business confidence pattern is very similar to the pattern for *industrial output*, which is just one component of GNP. (The seasonal peak in GNP in the fourth quarter is largely a reflection of buoyant retail business.)

Industrial output

We shall look at total output for production industries and at the particular characteristics of a specific industry, namely sulphuric acid.

Up to 1978, the *Monthly Digest of Statistics* published a monthly 'Index of Industrial Production'. More recently, a modified series 'Output of the Production Industries' has been recorded. Data in a seasonally *un*adjusted form have been published only since 1982. Consequently, total output was analysed for two rather short time periods:

Index of Industrial Production, 1975−78
Output of the Production Industries, 1982−84

The results are given in Figure 19.2a. In view of the brevity of these series, I have also reproduced in Figure 19.2b the seasonal pattern for earlier years. You can see that this is virtually identical to the pattern for industrial production in 1975−78.

The general patterns of output are very similar (from June onwards they are effectively identical). In recent years, part of the peak output in February and March has shifted to April and May. This may be a real effect, or it may reflect the change in definition of the series.

In any case, the general picture is fairly clear:

(a) a peak in output in February/March, about one month *ahead* of the corresponding peak in business confidence;
(b) a substantial decline in July/August, roughly *at the same time* as the trough in business confidence;
(c) a second peak in October/November, about a month *behind* the secondary peak in business confidence.

The magnitude of the effects is rather large: the August minimum is about 20 per cent below the February/March peak.

The second peak will include increased output in anticipation of the Christmas trade. We saw, in Chapter 10, the extent to which final sales are concentrated in the Christmas period.

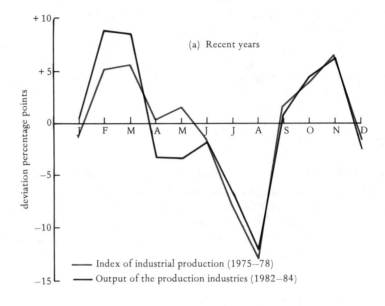

(a) Recent years

—— Index of industrial production (1975–78)
—— Output of the production industries (1982–84)

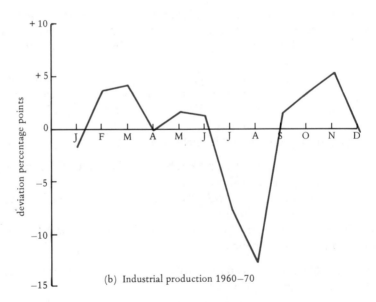

(b) Industrial production 1960–70

Fig. 19.2   Industrial output

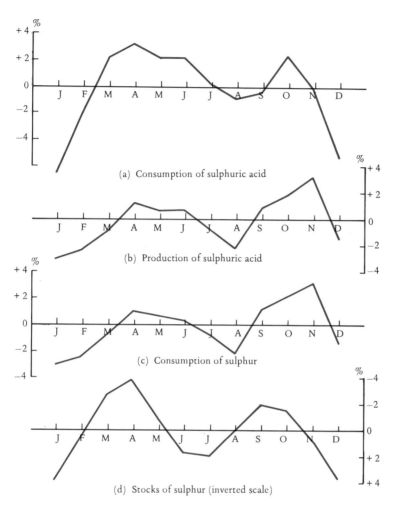

Fig. 19.3   **Consumption, production and stocks for sulphur and
sulphuric acid**

Any individual business is likely to have a seasonal pattern somewhat
different from these total industry results. One business for which the data are
readily available, and which can therefore be used for illustration, is sulphuric
acid. It is also a useful business to look at in its own right, since the
consumption of sulphuric acid is often regarded as a very good indicator of
economic activity.

In Figure 19.3 we start with the consumption of sulphuric acid and then see what this means, in turn, for sulphuric acid production, sulphur consumption and sulphur stocks.

Each point on these graphs has itself been plotted as a 3-month moving average. This helps to highlight the underlying pattern and to account for the fact that there are slightly different numbers of working days in each month. It does, however, mean that some fine detail is lost; in particular, it smooths out a brief dip in April, by averaging the results for that month with the more buoyant months of March and May. (If you refer back to Figure 19.2, you will see that this April dip is a general phenomenon.)

The general shape of the seasonal pattern is nevertheless similar to that for industrial output in total, except that the August minimum is less pronounced and the December/January minimum is much more pronounced.

At the foot of Figure 19.3 is a graph of seasonal variations in stocks of sulphur. This is plotted upside-down, so that low stocks are lined up with high levels of production and consumption.

All the graphs are of the same general shape as that for total industrial output (Figure 19.2). They are actually closer to the CBI business survey results than are the results for total output. In Figure 19.4, sulphur and sulphuric acid results are compared with corresponding CBI survey data; the strong similarities are immediately apparent. The only real difference is that actual output during the second peak (i.e. September to November) is more buoyant than would be expected from the survey results.

The fact that the actual output and stock graphs correspond fairly closely to the survey data is intriguing. The 'output expectations' poll asked about output prospects four months hence; the 'stocks' poll asked how the level of stocks compares to its normal or desired level at the *current time of the year*. It is impossible to escape the conclusion, already mentioned in Chapter 16, that business opinion about the future is largely a reflection of the state of business at the present time. It is also apparent that, in recording opinion on stock levels, businessmen in general are quite unaware of the seasonal variations which they might expect in their businesses. The exception to this general comment is that businessmen *are* aware, to some extent, that the surge in output and the reduction in stocks in the late autumn are partly temporary phenomena in anticipation of the Christmas trade.

In this book I can, of course, give only an introduction to seasonal patterns in output, based on aggregated statistics such as total industrial output for the UK economy. Each business really needs to analyse its own seasonal patterns for itself. I have therefore indicated in Appendix I how to go about doing that.

One output series which comes later in the book is that of energy production. I have treated this more as an *input* into other industries and activities.

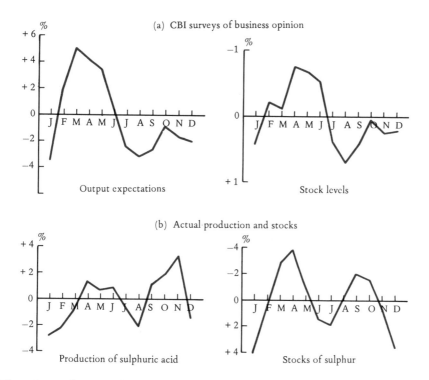

Fig. 19.4   **Comparison with CBI survey results**

TECHNICAL NOTE

Official statistics are quite often published in both 'unadjusted' and 'seasonally adjusted' form. If so – and if the seasonal variations are fairly consistent from one year to another – then these two series of published data can be used to obtain the seasonal pattern directly. This was possible in the case of the GNP data: the ratios of unadjusted to adjusted GNP figures for each quarter have been very consistent from one year to another in recent years. The seasonal deviations shown in Figure 19.1 were hence calculated simply by dividing the unadjusted values by the adjusted values.

20 Commodities

The most important input into business operations, whether industrial or service activities, is labour. We have already seen the seasonal patterns relating to jobs and incomes in Chapter 8. So we shall move on to look at the monthly variations in another important input, commodity prices. Since energy (especially oil) has had a special significance in recent years, this is dealt with separately in Chapter 21. The other key input is money; the cost of money (i.e. interest rates) is the subject of Chapter 22.

Before we look at the detailed results for commodity prices, I ought to make two general observations about the analysis.

(a) Commodities are traditionally quoted in US dollars. Hence the data are all based on dollar prices. By way of introduction, however, I shall show how sterling prices generally compare with those dollar prices.

(b) It is convenient to include, in this chapter, a number of products which are not exactly important raw material inputs into industry − for instance, eggs and potatoes. These patterns are also based on US dollar prices, for which the data were readily available. They should provide a good guide to the monthly variations which we should expect in Britain.

Sterling and dollar indices

The *Economist* regularly publishes price indices for various categories of raw materials. The categories are:

- all items
- food

- metals
- 'non-food agriculturals'

The last series has been produced only since 1982, when it replaced a slightly different series designated as 'fibres'. The main effect of this change was to introduce timber into the index; this was not included in the earlier 'fibres' index.

These price indices are given in both sterling and dollars, so we can start by comparing the seasonal patterns for prices in each of the two currencies. This comparison is shown in Figure 20.1. In fact, the patterns are quite similar, indicating that we can go on to look in detail at the individual raw materials priced in dollars, without introducing any real distortions for the UK importer. Excluding, for a moment, the 'non-food agriculturals', there is only one real difference between the two groups: the sterling price index falls relative to the dollar index in December and January. It would be reasonable to conclude from this that the pound is strong relative to the dollar in December and January. In Chapter 24, on exchange rates, we shall see that this is roughly confirmed, although the exchange rate data tend to suggest January and February as the period of strength for the pound. The close similarity between the two commodity series for the remainder of the year is useful confirmation of a later conclusion, namely that there are no other significant seasonal differences between the two currencies apart from those at the turn of the year.

I have excluded 'non-food agriculturals' from the above comments, because the analysis covered too short a time period. In fact, during that period, the pound must have been weaker, rather than stronger, at the turn of the year. This is confirmed by a detailed look at the computer print-out for exchange rates. As oil prices have weakened, so the relative strength of the pound against the dollar in winter has also diminished.

On the other hand, the exchange rate effect showed up particularly strongly when analysing the earlier 'fibres' series. Indeed, the strength of the pound in January and February was the most significant feature of those earlier series of fibres prices, conforming exactly to the pound v. dollar exchange rate pattern.

The close similarity between the two seasonal patterns (based, respectively, on pounds and dollars) has occurred despite the fact that the long-term trends have deviated quite sharply from each other due to longer-term changes in exchange rates.

Several of the patterns shown in Figure 20.1 reflect the familiar M factor. They *all* include the primary spring peak; the secondary peak, where it occurs, is generally very weak. In several instances there is no secondary peak at all, and the pattern is more nearly sinusoidal in shape (i.e. like the sine wave familiar in trigonometry).

Having established the general patterns, we shall go on to look at the main

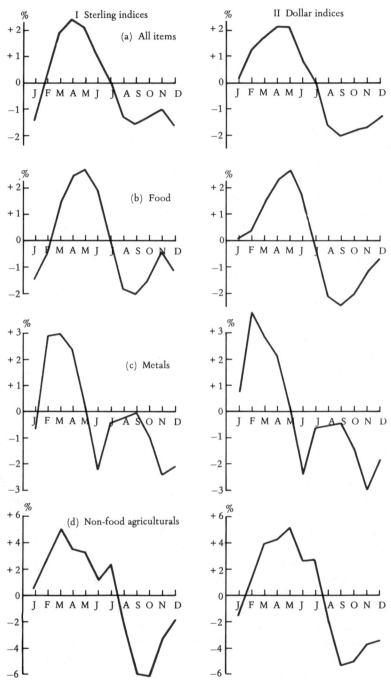

Fig. 20.1   Commodity price indices

Series:	Food (%)		Metals (%)		Non-food agriculturals (%)	
Weight in 'all items' index:	48.8		30.2		21.0	
Individual components:	Coffee	26.5	Aluminium	34.9	Timber	34.0
	Maize	12.1	Copper	32.3	Cotton	19.6
	Sugar	12.1	Nickel	10.8	Wool	18.2
	Soya beans	11.6	Tin	7.9	Rubber	14.2
	Cocoa	8.2	Zinc	7.5	Hides	7.1
	Soya meal	7.5	Lead	6.6	Soya beans	4.8
	Beef	6.8			Others	2.1
	Wheat	6.6				
	Lamb	2.4				
	Tea	2.2				
	Misc. oils	4.0				
		100%		100%		100%

Fig. 20.2   Constituents of the *Economist* **commodity indices**
Note: the weights assigned to each constituent are based on the total of imports into all OECD countries, not just the United States.

individual components. In Figure 20.2 the main constituents of the *Economist* indices are listed; seasonal patterns for these constituents will then be shown separately.

Food

The 'all items' pattern is influenced predominantly by food, which accounts for almost half of the total weight of the 'all items' index. Before looking at the individual components of the food index, we can first compare some of the seasonal patterns with a limited amount of work published elsewhere. The US journal *Cycles* contains regular contributions by Gertrude Shirk, who reports on the cyclic behaviour of a number of commodities. Two recent articles – one on eggs and one on soya beans – specifically describe the seasonal patterns which she has identified.

The comparison between her results and mine is shown in Figure 20.3. You can see that the *shapes* of the seasonal patterns are almost identical. Gertrude Shirk actually found greater amplitudes of seasonal change than I did. There

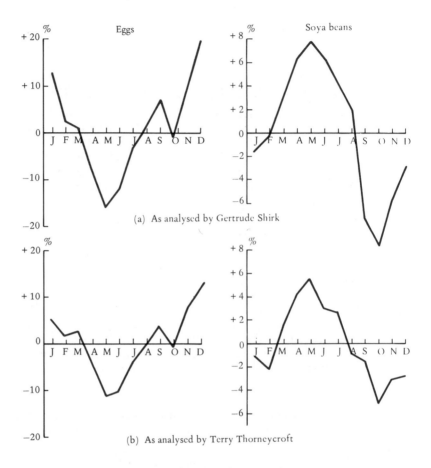

(a) As analysed by Gertrude Shirk

(b) As analysed by Terry Thorneycroft

Fig. 20.3   Comparison with other work on seasonality in commodity prices

are several reasons why this may have happened: (a) we may have taken different time periods for our respective analyses; (b) we may have used different sources of data; or (c) we may have used different mathematical techniques. The important feature, though, is that the shapes are so similar. It is always useful to have an independent corroboration of one's analysis, and I was very pleased to find such a marked similarity in the patterns which we had each calculated.

It is therefore with added confidence that we can proceed to illustrate the patterns calculated for a range of individual commodities. These results are shown in Figures 20.4 to 20.6 inclusive.

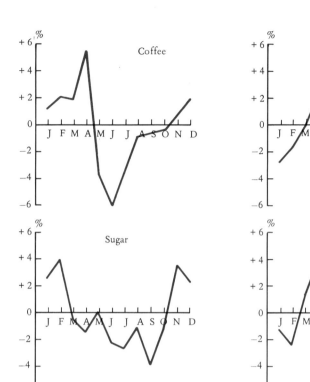

Fig. 20.4   Food prices

It was not always possible to match exactly the individual components of the *Economist* food index, but you will see that I have included most of them. All of these individual charts are based on prices in US dollars.

Food prices fall, usually quite sharply, at harvest time; they then rise again during the next growing season as stocks from the previous harvest are depleted. Although the general shapes are the same (the 'sinusoidal' patterns mentioned earlier), the timing of the harvests differs considerably, of course. The seasonal variations are all quite large, which is no more than you would expect from something which depends predominantly on the natural cycle of the seasons. The largest seasonal variations in all the foods which I analysed occurred with potatoes: the price in spring is something like half as much again as the price at which they can be bought in the autumn.

The average effect of all of these individual price variations is the smooth curve of dollar prices shown in Figure 20.1; these average variations are naturally much smaller than the variations for any single food item. The average pattern for US prices is similar to the seasonal pattern in UK food prices which we saw in Figure 9.2c. In both countries, food prices tend to be

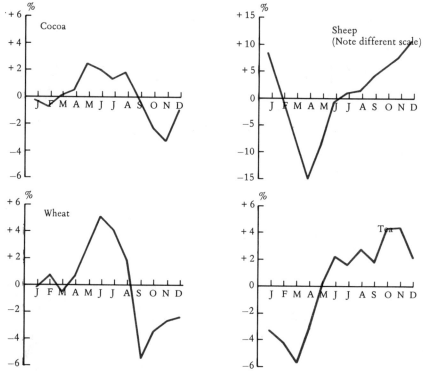

Fig. 20.5   Food prices (continued)

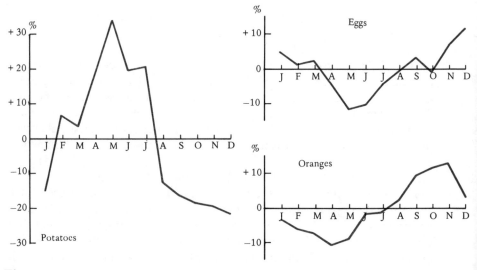

Fig. 20.6   Other foods not included in the index

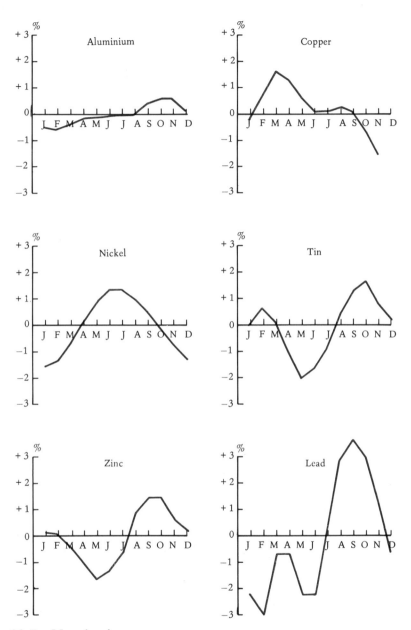

Fig. 20.7   Metal prices

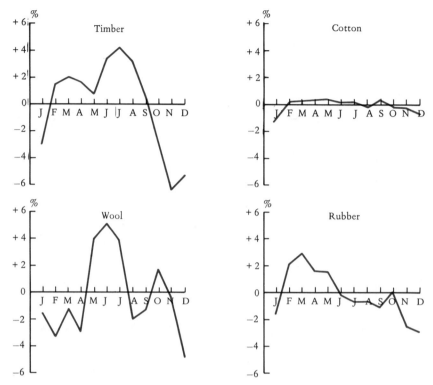

Fig. 20.8   Prices of 'non-food agriculturals'

rather higher in the first half of the year and then fall relatively sharply between June and August.

Metals

The month-to-month variations in metal prices are, not surprisingly, very much less than we have just found with food; in fact, much of the variation which we shall see could be due to purely random factors. Nevertheless, individual patterns are given in Figure 20.7 for each of the six constituents of the *Economist* metals price index. The monthly variation in the index is actually rather higher than you would expect just by averaging out the variations in the individual metals; the index must be based on rather different price series to the ones which I have used.

Despite this caveat, the primary peak in the index is clearly attributable mainly to the seasonal peak in copper prices. Other metals which have either a lower seasonal variation (aluminium) or a much lower weight in the index (tin, zinc, lead) contribute to the secondary peak in the autumn.

It would be a full study in its own right to relate these price variations to the seasonal variations in the supply and demand for each metal. Not that supply and demand are necessarily the only factors: until recently, the price of tin was artificially maintained by the International Tin Council. Why this artificially high level should have been especially high in October, I do not know; however, it may be no coincidence that October was precisely the month in 1985 when the laws of supply and demand finally broke the Council.

Non-food agriculturals

The recent introduction of timber as a component – indeed, a dominant component – of the index has had a pronounced effect on the seasonal pattern shown at the foot of Figure 20.1. Wool and rubber also show significant effects (Figure 20.8), whereas the price of cotton is much more stable from one month to another. The combined effect of timber, wool and rubber is to give a rather extended period of high prices in the spring and summer, with prices falling sharply in autumn (mainly due to timber) and remaining low in the winter.

One very important raw material which has not been included in this chapter is oil; this is the main subject of the next chapter.

21 Oil and energy

Total energy consumption is, as you would expect, roughly a mirror image of the temperature pattern. The energy pattern given in Figure 21.1 is actually based on just three years of production data, subsequent to a change in definition in the published output statistics. Also, the published series is for 'energy and water supply'. Nevertheless, the seasonal effects are very consistent and they will be dominated by the energy component.

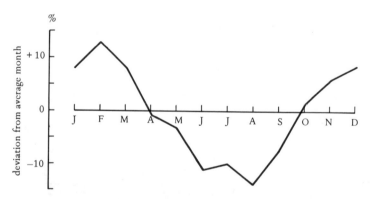

Fig. 21.1   UK output: energy (and water supply)

A similar seasonal pattern of energy consumption will apply in the United States, and the price of crude petroleum at oil wells in that country (Figure 21.2) closely parallels the energy consumption curve. This is not true of the 'spot' price of North Sea oil, for the more limited period of mid-1980– mid-

1985. These seasonal effects fluctuate much more, from month to month and also from year to year for each month. What is intriguing is that the pattern *anticipates* rather than *parallels* energy consumption. It suggests that the marginal demand for oil, which is affecting spot prices, is related more to stock-building rather than to final demand; this stock-building takes two forms: (i) that carried out in *anticipation* of a forthcoming winter peak in demand; and (ii) that carried out in mid-year to *replenish* stocks depleted in the winter.

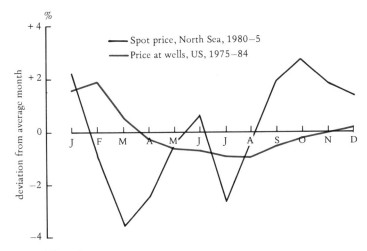

Fig. 21.2   Oil prices

I have deliberately chosen a period of time which starts *after* the second OPEC oil 'shock' of 1979, so as to present a picture which might be more representative of future events. As a result, I haven't really analysed a sufficiently long period. Within that short period, however, perhaps the most surprising feature of the spot oil price is that the average seasonal effects are really not all that large (and they are also very inconsistent, which is one reason why the average deviations are so small).

Part of the process of anticipation, which I mentioned earlier, is the expectation of a low temperature level in the winter. If the winter turns out to be relatively mild, then (even though the actual winter temperatures are obviously still lower than the temperatures in other months) demand will not be as high as anticipated, and stocks will accordingly deplete at a lower rate than expected. A considerable part of the variations in spot prices depends, therefore, not so much on the *actual* variations in monthly temperatures, as on whether those temperatures are higher or lower than would be *expected* for the time of the year.

The results of this seasonal analysis are entirely consistent with the collapse in oil prices from January to March 1986. We have seen that it is the weakest time of the year for oil prices, despite the fact that consumption is high at that time. (Clearly, had the analysis been extended to include 1986, the February/March minimum would have come out as being very much more pronounced.) You will see, from this analysis, that I was not at all surprised to see the oil price collapse in the winter; most people were probably expecting a fall – but not until the onset of summer.

The difference between reality and expectation raises the intriguing possibility of a speculative opportunity. The general *expectation* is for spot oil prices to fall at the end of winter, i.e. from March to early summer; the *reality* is just the opposite: prices tend to rise during that period as diminished stocks are replenished. This would seem to offer the chance of making quite a good profit, by buying oil forward in March for delivery in June. It is not my real intention to encourage you to gamble in this way – so don't blame me if you end up having to take physical delivery of 100,000 tons of oil in the middle of summer!

22 Interest rates

Probably more has been written on interest rate variations than on any other aspect of seasonality, as far as business is concerned. Even so, there is not a very extensive literature on the subject. Some of the more significant work is described in the next chapter.

By way of introduction, there are three general points which I should make concerning interest rates:

(a) Like any other price in a free market, the price of money (which is what an interest rate is) depends on the balance between supply and demand. The *demand* for money is the more likely to follow a consistent seasonal pattern (which, in turn, will be related to the strong seasonal patterns in the demands of government, agriculture, industry, commerce and tourism). The *supply* of money can be more easily and quickly turned on or off by governments and by banks. If there is a deliberate policy to try to match demand to supply, then the seasonal variations are likely to be less than when a *laissez-faire* situation prevails in the supply of money to the banking system. The point I wish to emphasize is that the seasonal patterns which we shall see do not necessarily reflect patterns in either demand or supply, but in the balance between the two.

(b) Just as we may not always be able to disentangle supply and demand influences, so we cannot necessarily distinguish between cause and effect. For instance, do lower interest rates cause business activity to increase at certain times of the year, or do interest rates fall because business activity has declined?

(c) A third dilemma is whether to regard low interest rates as a 'good thing' or as a 'bad thing'. It is not universally the case that low interest rates are beneficial: for many people, certainly those living largely off fixed investment income, a sharp fall in real interest rates may be a minor disaster. I understand that, in the United States, the investment income of individuals actually exceeds their debt interest payments, so that they are apparently better off if interest rates rise. However, even for such people, falling interest rates often mean an increase in the capital value of their investments. Even when it doesn't (e.g. in the UK, building society shares), it will generally mean that a fixed amount of capital is being less quickly eroded by inflation.

On balance – and certainly from a businessman's point of view – it seems sensible to regard low interest rates as being 'good'. The consequence of this is that the seasonal patterns in this chapter are plotted upside down: a peak in the curve is indicative of low interest rates, a trough high interest rates. Another way of looking at this is to imagine that the curves represent, not the level of interest rates, but the *value* of the corresponding interest-bearing stocks. We shall see that this then provides a more direct visual comparison with the patterns for other variable-priced investments, such as shares. However, the results for Australia and Japan will illustrate why it is not always obvious that low interest rates are a good thing: in both countries, months in which interest rates are low tend to coincide with months in which both share prices and business confidence are also low.

With that necessary preamble, we can now move on to look at the actual results. To anticipate what follows, we shall find very clear, consistent patterns for the UK but not for some other countries.

UK interest rates

Figure 22.1 shows the seasonal variation in short-term rates (as measured by 3-month Treasury Bills), shown in relation to the seasonal pattern of business confidence (as measured by the CBI survey of output expectations). Two features stand out from the diagram.

In the first place, the interest rates graph exhibits the familiar 'M' shape in a quite pronounced fashion. Given that the average interest rate over the 10-year period 1975–84 was about 10 per cent, then the difference between March and November represents on average an interest rate differential of over one percentage point. This is not only statistically significant, but also quite substantial. In seven years out of nine, interest rates fell from November to the following March; on the two occasions when interest rates rose during this period, the amount of the rise was very small.

Secondly, the interest rate graph and the business confidence graph are almost identical for the first half of the year; in the second half, the secondary

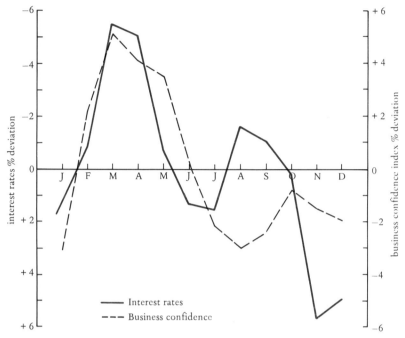

**Fig. 22.1   Short-term interest rates (UK Treasury Bills) shown
against a background of business confidence**

peak in the (inverted) interest rate graph leads the confidence graph by about
2 months.

Treasury Bills are representative of very short-term interest rates. Figure
22.2 depicts patterns for securities with longer times to maturity; also,
undated stocks which offer a continuous yield out to infinity. These series
start with 1977 data (rather than 1975), to avoid difficulties which would
otherwise have been encountered because of a change in the basis of the
published statistics. Again, the 'M' shape is very obvious.

As the period to maturity increases, there is a tendency for the timing of
maximum interest rates to move forwards a little in time, i.e.

3-month Treasury Bills	highest in November
0–5-Year Bonds	highest in January
5+-Year Bonds	highest in Feburary

Perhaps surprisingly, the patterns for UK industrial share prices (Figures
17.2 and 17.3) are more similar to that for the *short*-term interest rates than to
those for longer-term rates.

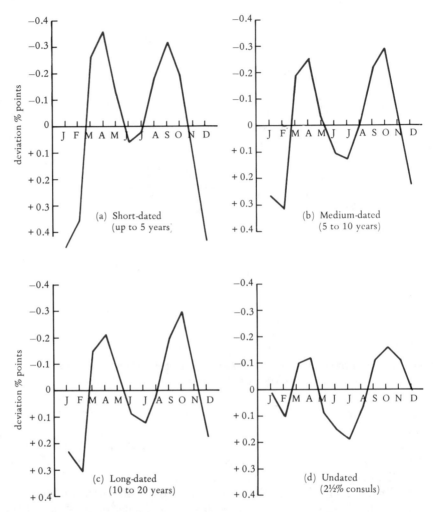

Fig. 22.2   British Government securities of different dates to maturity

More obviously from the graphs, we can see that the magnitude of the seasonal variations diminishes somewhat as the period to maturity increases. In the next chapter, I shall tell you about some earlier work by Stanley Diller, on US interest rates, in which the same feature was noted; Diller concluded that this effect was to be expected.

Before moving on, though, I should like to show you the actual interest rate patterns for two particular years, 1973 and 1979. These were the two years which will be remembered for the two economic 'shocks' caused by massive increases in oil prices. You might well have expected that such shock waves would have completely submerged any underlying seasonal variations in interest rates. In fact, exactly the reverse happened: you can see from Figure 22.3 that interest rates in those years show the M-factor very clearly (superimposed, in both years, on a strong upward trend in rates during the course of the year).

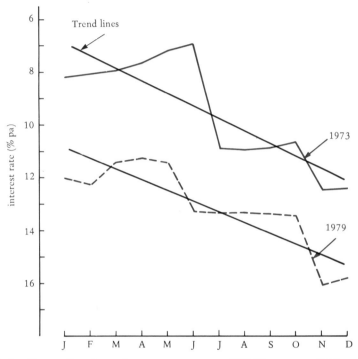

Fig. 22.3   Two oil crises: interest rates on UK Treasury Bills

We can go back further, before the first OPEC crisis, to see whether or not the 'M' shaped pattern of interest rates is relatively new. Figure 22.4 shows the patterns both before and after the traumatic events of 1973. You can see that the patterns for short-term interest rates are very similar in the two periods; the 'M' factor was at work in the 1960s just as much as in recent years. The picture for long-term rates is not so consistent. The mid-year rise in interest rates (i.e. a decline in the value of stocks) was certainly there in the earlier period; however, December and January were rather more favourable months than we might have expected. In fact, this long-term bond pattern for the earlier period is actually more similar to that for the United States than

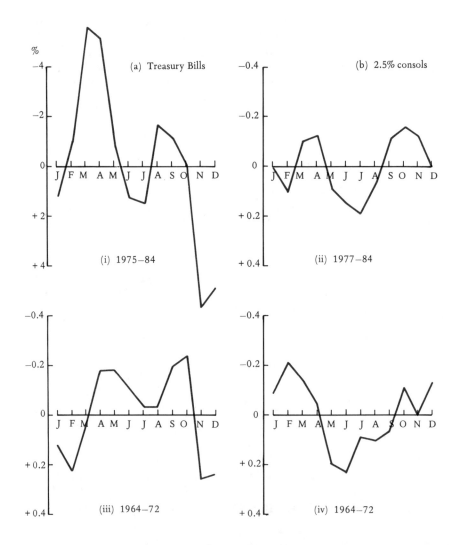

Fig. 22.4   Interest rates at two different time periods

to either (a) UK short-term interest rates in the same period; or (b) UK long-term rates in the more recent period.

US interest rates

In recent years, that is since 1975, there really hasn't been much similarity between UK and US interest rates. The underlying trends are shown in Figure 22.5. Whilst these may look similar superficially, in fact the turning points in the two curves bear no clear relationship to each other.

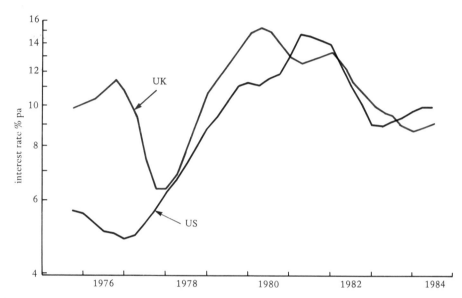

Fig. 22.5   Trends in UK and US short-term interest rates (3-month Treasury Bills)

When we come to the seasonal patterns (Figure 22.6), we see that they are, if anything, mirror images of each other. (In practice, the US pattern would have shown no significant seasonal variation at all had it not been for the results of a sharp change in interest rates in 1980.)

The pattern of *long-term* interest rates in the US has actually changed considerably over the years. Figure 22.7 shows the results of analysing data given by Sidney Homer, in his comprehensive study *A History of Interest Rates*. He gives monthly data going back as far as 1900, although he did not himself analyse the seasonal effects. I could find no significant seasonal effects in data prior to 1956. The pattern for 1966–75 is very similar indeed to one found by C.W. Sealey for the latter half of that period.

Sealey's results are given in the next chapter. That chapter also provides a likely clue to why the interest rates in the UK and US are completely different. In fact, as noted above, they seem if anything to be mirror images of each other. This would actually be quite consistent with one of the conclusions which other people have drawn, and which we shall come back to

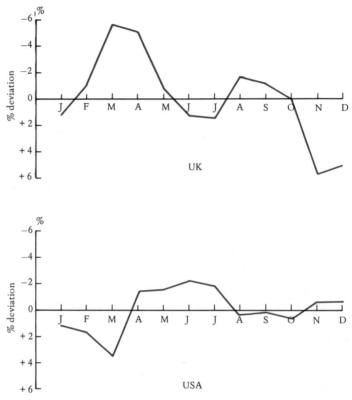

**Fig. 22.6   Comparison between seasonal patterns for UK and US
short-term interest rates (Treasury Bills)**

in the next chapter. American authors comment that the increasing demand for money in the later months of the year is, in the United States, accompanied by a more 'accommodative' stance by the Federal Reserve. In other words, the *supply* of money is allowed to increase to offset, at least in part, the greater demands at that time of the year. From Figure 22.6 we might conclude that occasionally, the US authorities 'overshoot' the mark and inject more than enough money into their banking system.

Since UK interest rates have seasonal patterns more closely in line with other economic variables, we might also conclude that the UK authorities adopt a more 'passive' role in respect of money supply.

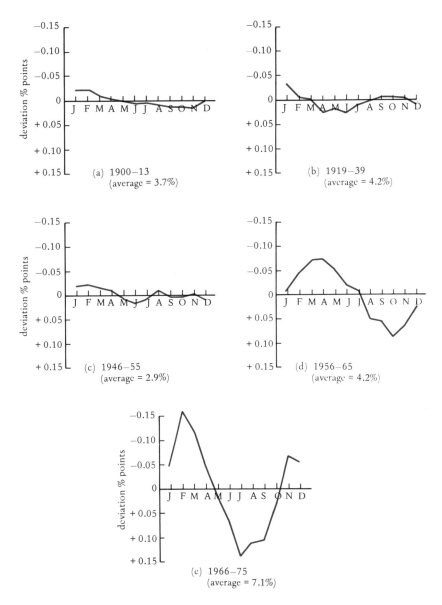

Fig. 22.7   US corporate and municipal long-term bonds

(Source of data: *A History of Interest Rates* by S. Homer, 1977)

Pacific area

We finally look at what has happened in two of the main countries in the Pacific area: Japan and Australia (Figure 22.8). In line with the approach we have taken earlier, the chart for Australia is displaced relative to northern hemisphere countries: June (rather than January) is taken as the start of the year. If the patterns for the US are difficult to interpret, those for Australia and Japan are even more confusing.

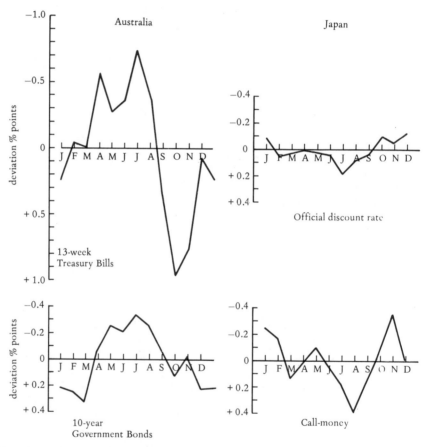

Fig. 22.8   Interest rates – Pacific area

Interest rates in Australia are low, not in the spring, but in their mid-summer. This pattern is not only different from any others which we have seen for interest rates; it is also quite different from the pattern for Australian share prices (Figure 17.8). Moreover, the business confidence pattern for Australia (Figure 16.11) is almost exactly the opposite of what you would expect from the interest rate pattern.

Japan, also, shows no seasonal similarity between interest rates and stock market prices. Although the monthly variations in interest rates are not so pronounced, some of the particular features are very consistent. The call-money rate for August exceeded its 12-month moving average in every single year of the analysis; the November rate was below the moving average for every single year. Given that there is such a consistent fall in interest rates from August to November, it is particularly surprising that the Tokyo stock exchange tends to fall (relatively) rather than rise strongly during this same period. The inscrutable Japanese again!

Summing up

The analysis of interest rate variations has several of the general features that we found with share prices. The UK patterns are very consistent and similar to other seasonal patterns (e.g. in share prices and business confidence); the US patterns are much weaker or even non-existent; Australia and Japan are very confusing!

23 The history of the seasonal analysis of interest rates

Very little work has been reported on seasonal factors in business life. Most of the work which *has* been reported concerns US interest rates.

Like so many other things, the analysis of interest rate seasonality was actually a British invention which was left to the Americans to develop. The story starts with a study by W. Stanley Jevons, published in 1866, entitled *Frequent Autumnal Pressure in the Money Market, and the Action of the Bank of England.*

Interest in the subject in Britain continued up to the end of the last century, since when it appears to have disappeared from sight. Meanwhile, the scene switches to America, whence have come a number of relevant studies. We shall look at the more important ones in this chapter.

In the process, we shall see that Jevons's observation about autumnal pressure was equally applicable to the US. The other consistent theme is the difference between long- and short-term bonds: seasonal variations in *long*-term interest rates have always been relatively low or, at times, non-existent.

The starting point of the American studies is an article by E.W. Kemmerer, entitled 'Seasonal Variations in the New York Money Markets'. This was published in 1911; in fact, it appeared in the very first issue of the *American Economic Review*.

At that time, it was common for interest rates to swing quite violently. Within a single year they would change from a low of around 2 per cent up to a brief, sharp peak of perhaps 6 per cent. These peaks typically occurred during the first weeks of January and July, and were associated with half-yearly interest payments. Apart from these rather artificial peaks, the money markets tended to be 'stringent' in late autumn and early winter.

This is, of course, very much in line with Jevons's earlier work in the UK;

as we have seen from the title of his paper, he found consistent monetary pressures in the autumn. This will be a repetitive theme of the subsequent story: for over 100 years, up to 1970, the last quarter of the year has consistently been the one in which demands for money in the US have tended to outstrip supply. We saw, in the previous chapter, that November and December are *still* the peak months for interest rates in the UK.

Kemmerer ascribed the seasonal variations to:

> ... seasonal flows of money into and out of New York in response to the demands of agriculture, transportation and foreign trade, to the servicing of outstanding debt and equity securities, to the year-end 'window dressing' of balance sheets [even then!] ... and to the currency needs of holiday periods.

Kemmerer's study was one of those which preceded the creation of the US Federal Reserve in 1914; indeed, one of the Fed's principal objectives was precisely to smooth out the more violent seasonal swings, by the appropriate injection of adequate funds when seasonal demand for money was high.

Commenting on the creation of the Fed, Sidney Homer (in his book *A History of Interest Rates*) states:

> ... the seasonal fluctuations in rates were smoothed out, so that short-term debtors no longer stood in fear of the demands of farmers each fall, or the demands of the Christmas trade, or of dividend dates.

Frederick K. Macauley also emphasized the financial demands of farmers in the autumn. In 1938 he wrote 'Some Theoretical Problems Suggested by the Movement of Interest Rates, Bond Yields and Stock Prices in the United States since 1856'. His explanation for the pre-Fed seasonal variations mirrors that of Kemmerer and Homer:

> The demand for funds in the country districts for the paying of farm labour, the storing of grain and the moving of produce to the primary markets calls for an outflow of funds from the financial centres to the interior. At the same time, the demand from producing and manufacturing enterprises which are making ready for the fall trade becomes very heavy, thus bringing added pressure to bear on the financial markets.

So, was the Fed successful in relieving these seasonal pressures on the money markets?

If you turn to Figure 23.1, you will see that (according to Macauley) there was still quite a large rise in interest rates in the autumn, at least in the first year after the Fed was founded.

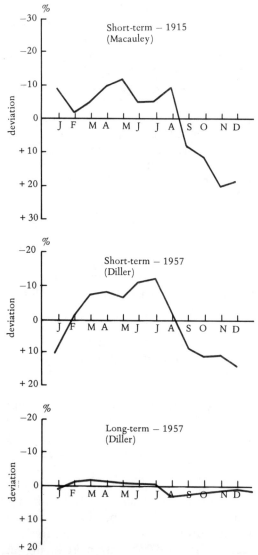

Fig. 23.1   Some historical data given by Stanley Diller (with scales inverted)

Reproduced by kind permission of the National Institute of Economic Research, Inc., from *Seasonal Variations in Interest Rates*, by Stanley Diller, Occasional Paper 108, Copyright 1969 by National Bureau of Economic Research, Inc. (New York).

This actually seems to be in conflict with two very recent analyses of the Fed's initial impact. Although both studies were published as recently as 1986, they analyse events just before and after 1914.

These recent papers are by, respectively, J.A. Miron and T.A. Clark; the full references are given in Appendix II. The fact that these two studies have both come out recently may indicate a re-awakening of more general interest in the subject of seasonality. Both authors also consider the relationships between interest rate seasonality and the onset of financial panics – a subject which I approach in Chapter 28.

Both of these recent authors refer to a significant reduction in – or, even, disappearance of – interest rate seasonality from around 1914 to 1929; as to the cause, they come up with quite different conclusions. Miron finds that the changes after 1914 were consistent with a theoretical model of how the Fed's actions should have successfully stabilized the situation. Clark, on the other hand, casts doubts on the role of the Fed in smoothing the seasonal variations. This he does for two reasons: (a) the same smoothing effect also occurred in other countries from 1914; (b) the action of the Fed, in increasing money supply to counteract seasonal pressures, was not actually evident until 1919 – three years *after* (according to Clark) the strong seasonality in interest rates disappeared.

After this lull from 1914 to 1929, some degree of seasonality reappeared. It has persisted for most of the time since then, at least up to the 1970s.

Data for the period 1932–61 were studied by T.E. Holland; it formed the subject of a 1963 Duke University thesis 'Forecasting Interest Rate Movements: Time Series Analyses and Functional Relationships'. A microfilm of this thesis is buried in the archives of the London Business School. It was a very thorough analysis: I hope that he was awarded his degree!

Holland's results were very much in line with what we have already seen for the period up to 1914:

(a)   the peak in short-term interest rates was generally in the period September to January;
(b)   very little seasonal variation was found in long-term bonds.

There is a much more easily accessible study which largely overlaps that of Holland. It is a book by Stanley Diller, entitled *The Seasonal Variation of Interest Rates*, published in 1969 by the National Bureau of Economic Research in New York. This is a very good starting point for the study of the period since the Second World War.

Diller (like Holland) used the X-11 method, which enabled him to obtain estimates of the seasonal pattern for each individual year. He found a consistent pattern of seasonal variations, but the *amplitude* of those variations changed considerably over the study period, reaching a peak around 1957.

This is the year which is illustrated in Figure 23.1. (Note the similarity with the pattern given by Macauley for 1915 – forty years earlier.)

Short-term rates in America rose to a peak in December and reached a trough in July; variations in long-term rates were much less pronounced. In fact, the degree of seasonality was found to decline steadily according to the number of years to maturity of the bonds.

A possibly surprising feature is that the seasonal effect was most pronounced when the underlying level of interest rates was itself oscillating fairly wildly (see Figure 23.2). At times when interest rates were rising slowly and smoothly, the seasonal pattern was almost non-existent; on the other hand, the 1957–8 period of maximum seasonality was a time when the general level of interest rates was falling fast. This is surprising, on the face of it, because we might have expected such large long-term changes to swamp any seasonal factors. However, it is less surprising to us now that we have seen

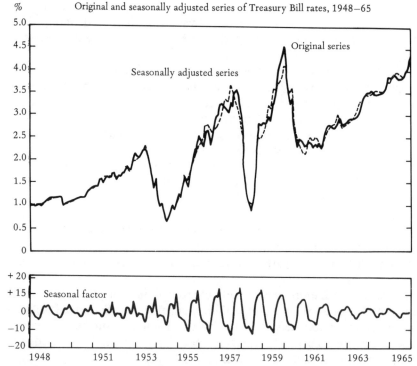

Fig. 23.2   Diller's results for short-term interest rates

Reproduced by kind permission of the National Institute of Economic Research, Inc., from pages 42 and 66 of *Seasonal Variations in Interest Rates*, by Stanley Diller, Occasional Paper 108, Copyright 1969 by National Bureau of Economic Research, Inc. (New York).

(Figures 16.2 and 22.3) a similar situation with both business confidence and UK interest rates.

Although Diller does not comment on this point, his conclusions on the underlying reasons for the seasonality may also help to explain why the seasonal factor is most pronounced at times of greatest underlying change.

It is all to do, of course (as we have already seen), with the operations of the Federal Reserve. Diller found that the *demand* for money was the main driving force; the *supply* of money tended to follow the same seasonal pattern, but with a smaller amplitude. In other words, money supply was adjusted to reflect to some extent (but not completely) the seasonal changes in demand; these adjustments damped down the effects of the demand variations but did not eliminate them entirely. Presumably, it was easier for the Federal Reserve to respond accurately to seasonal demand changes in periods of relatively stable rates, more so than when interest rates were fluctuating wildly.

As to the underlying causes of seasonal variations in the demand for money in the US, Diller lists several without coming to any firm conclusions:

> What, then, are the present sources of seasonal influence on the demand for credit? These sources are likely to be found in wholesale and retail trade; government fiscal activity, particularly short-term borrowing in autumn to close the gap between tax revenues and expenditures; corporate demand for credit to finance tax and dividend payments in the final quarter of the year, which may be regarded as an increased demand for credit or as a diminished supply of funds that at other times are available to finance government and trade debt; and no doubt other factors as well.(p.5)

Before looking at more recently published work, it is worth quoting Diller on the general subject of seasonal analysis. Despite the fact that he was using fairly sophisticated mathematical analyses, he emphasized that there is still much judgement involved in deciding whether a significant pattern exists or not.

With that comment in mind, it is intriguing to look back at some articles which appeared in the mid-1970s, in the journal *The Review of Economics and Statistics*. There was quite a heated debate about the significance or otherwise of seasonal variations in interest rates. It was initiated by an article in the February 1975 issue by James R. Barth and James T. Bennett: they concluded that there was *no* significant seasonal effect when monthly average interest rates were analysed for the period 1947–66.

In response, several other articles appeared in the February 1977 issue of that journal. These later articles reported that the seasonal effects *were* significant. One of the biggest criticisms of the Barth and Bennett analysis was their failure to correct for the underlying trends in interest rates over the period of study.

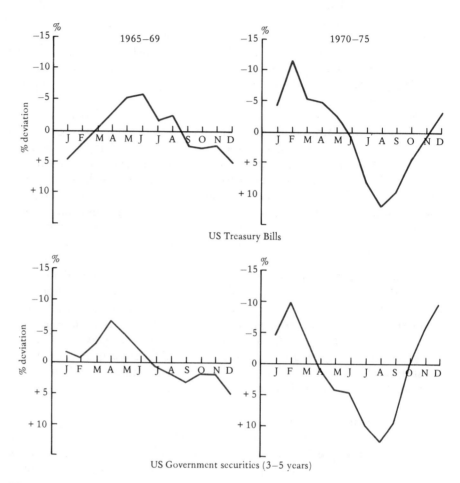

US Treasury Bills

US Government securities (3–5 years)

Fig. 23.3   Sealey's results for US interest rates, 1965 – 75

The whole argument revolved around some detailed points of statistical analysis. These are no doubt of great interest to statisticians, but I do feel that the debate obscured rather than illuminated the real nature of the seasonal variations.

Diller's earlier work is much more relevant to the approach adopted in this book. In the same vein, results published by Sealey in *Business Economics* are worth recording. Sealey studied the period from 1965 to 1975; this period conveniently bridges the gap between Diller's work and the results presented in this book.

A particular feature of the results was the observation of a significant change in the seasonal pattern around 1970. Consequently, he analysed the data for two separate time periods, 1965–69 and 1970–75. Some of the results are shown in Figure 23.3.

The results for 1965–69 are similar in shape to Diller's, but with a smaller amplitude. However, from 1970 onwards, a quite different pattern emerged. This is the first time we find that interest rates peaked other than in the last quarter of the year. Sealey comments:

> The general seasonal pattern of interest rates for the 1950s and 1960s closely resembles the pattern for the 1965–69 period, where the seasonal peak occurred in December. The most common and reasonable explanation for this seasonal pattern is that changes in the demand relative to the supply of credit during the latter part of each year, which are caused by seasonal borrowing and currency drains, were the primary seasonal influence on interest rates. However, the general tightness of credit during the end of each year appears to have diminished in importance as a problem in money and capital markets. The period of primary seasonal credit tightness appears to have shifted from the end of each year to the third quarter of each year.

This shift is clearly illustrated in Figure 23.3. Sealey then goes on to offer the following analysis of the causes of the seasonal effects, and also of the changes that took place around 1970. I can't honestly say that I understand what all this means, but I ought to include some conclusions from such a serious study of the question:

> It is difficult to determine the exact causes of the changes in seasonal movements in interest rates. There are, however, some casual observations that can be made concerning the problem.
> . . . when borrowing from the Federal Reserve was seasonally analysed, the results indicate that seasonal changes in this variable *have* occurred that are similar to the changes found for the interest rate series. The results for the 1970–75 subperiod indicate large increases in seasonal borrowing with a pronounced seasonal peak occurring in the third quarter. The large amount of seasonal borrowing, which in the past took place at the end of each year, has diminished.

> An analysis of the Federal Reserve's holdings of securities indicates that the Federal Reserve has not attempted to offset the seasonal fluctuations in US Government deposits at commercial banks but has instead concentrated on reacting to Treasury Deposits at the Federal Reserve. It appears, therefore, that a great deal of the third quarter seasonal tightness in money and capital markets is caused by government deposit flows, which force

financial institutions to enter money markets to borrow funds to compensate for the outflows. Interest rates are thus forced up when the demand for funds increases and no corresponding supply is forthcoming from the monetary authorities.

Sealey also makes the general observation:

A search of recent literature reveals no discussion of the importance of seasonality in interest rate forecasting. It appears, therefore, that many forecasters and other analysts who monitor interest rate movements have failed to consider seasonal variations.

In more recent years there has been a renewed interest in the question; however, as we have seen, this interest largely focuses on a renewed analysis of old historical data.

Summary

The really violent seasonal swings in US interest rates have been kept very much in check since the Federal Reserve was set up in 1914. Nevertheless, more modest but still significant seasonal effects have persisted for much of the time since then.

One dominant theme characterized the seasonal pattern for over 100 years up to 1970: short-term interest rates were typically high from September to January.

However, in the 1970s the peak occurred more typically in the third quarter of the year. Finally, my own analysis (reported in the previous chapter) indicates that the seasonal effect for the USA has largely disappeared altogether in recent years.

The earlier pattern in the US is not all that different from the picture we saw for the UK (Figures 22.1, 22.2a and 22.4). Short-dated UK bills and bonds tend to have an interest rate peak in the period November to January. Unlike the US experience, this UK pattern is still evident in very recent data. It would seem that the UK authorities have been less interested (or less successful) than their transatlantic counterparts in matching supply and demand. It is perhaps no coincidence that UK economists have also shown less interest than their American colleagues in the analysis of these seasonal variations. Meanwhile, in the latter half of 1986 Dr Henry Kaufman in the United States was quoted as saying that 'seasonal strains on the banking system will require the Fed to supply a generous volume of reserves in the coming weeks'. These seasonal pressures are clearly much better appreciated on the other side of the Atlantic.

There is some evidence of a renewed interest in interest rate seasonality. There could be considerable value in someone carrying out a detailed study of UK interest rate variations, in much greater depth than has been possible (in the previous chapter) for this more general compendium of seasonal factors.

24   Exchange rates

Exchange rates are notoriously difficult to forecast. I once studied the track records of several professional forecasters and found that none of them produced results which were any better than could be achieved by using the proverbial pin. Fortunately, our task is not to *forecast* exchange rates, but to analyse actual historical data, in order to detect any seasonal effects in the value of the pound; that is, how much it will buy of various other currencies at different times of the year.

In fact, in only a few cases were there any effects which were really significant. Nevertheless, so long as we remember not to assign too much credibility to the precise numbers, some general messages do emerge.

In this chapter we shall look both at exchange rates themselves and at the 3-month forward margins. The latter indicate the premium or discount, as a percentage per annum, required in order to take delivery of the foreign currency in 3 months' time. Figure 24.1 illustrates both of these series of results for the pound in relation to the Swiss franc, with any seasonal effects removed by plotting 12-month moving averages. The long-term trend for several decades has been for the pound to fall against the franc; however, the period of our study includes the years 1979 and 1980, during which the pound strengthened against all currencies because of Britain's self-sufficiency in oil. Even during this period, the pound was at a discount against the franc in the forward markets.

Month-to-month deviations from the 12-month moving averages are very erratic. In order to show up any underlying seasonal patterns more clearly, the monthly deviations themselves have been based on 3-month moving averages. For instance, the monthly deviation for February has been taken as the average of the deviations for January, February and March. Smoothing

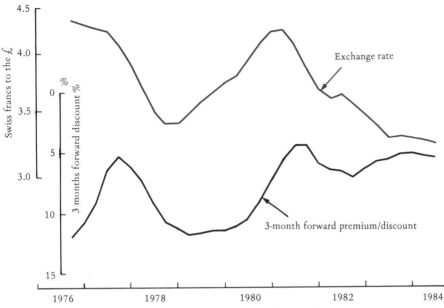

Fig. 24.1   Pound v. Swiss franc – 12-month moving averages

the seasonal pattern in this way inevitably risks losing some of the fine detail of that pattern. In fact, a study of the results shows that this smoothing process has obscured just one particularly interesting feature. In almost all of the examples analysed, the pound was actually lower in December and higher in January than shown on the graphs, sometimes by quite appreciable amounts; the same comment applies to its 3-month forward margins.

The rather erratic movements of the seasonal factors made it more difficult than usual to check the computer output for any errors which may have arisen in entering the data. However, I did come across one error which turned out to emanate from the Bank of England, no less. This is the only time that I have found any bank, never mind the Bank of England, put a 'plus' sign where there should have been a 'minus'!

Trade-weighted exchange rate

The general pattern of the pound over the course of a year is best illustrated by the 'trade-weighted index'. This is the exchange rate compared to a 'basket' of other currencies, weighted in proportion to the extent of trade between the UK and the various countries represented in the index. The annual average value of this index varied from 79 to 99 over the study period (1976–84).

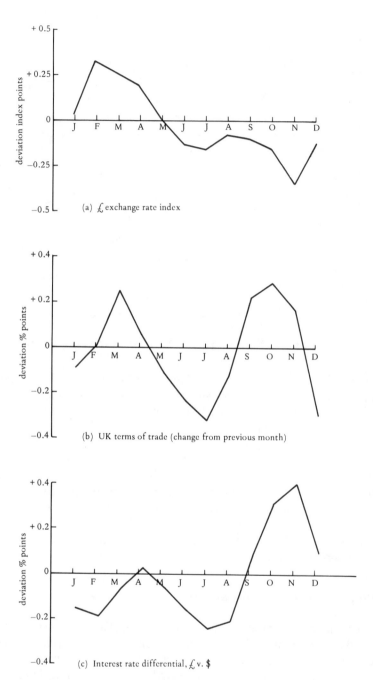

(a) £ exchange rate index

(b) UK terms of trade (change from previous month)

(c) Interest rate differential, £ v. $

Fig. 24.2   Exchange rate index of the pound

Figure 24.2a shows how this index varies during the course of an average year. In practice, few years can really be described as 'average'.

The pound tends to start the year relatively strongly (remember that the graph undercalls the January figures), to have a further period of relative strength in late summer, and then to end the year on a weak note.

The other graphs shown in Figure 24.2 are of two series which I thought might go some way to explain the seasonal pattern of exchange rate movements. The 'terms of trade' measures the relative price of exports from the UK, compared to the price of imported goods. There does seem to be a very close similarity between the two graphs, with the 'terms of trade' leading exchange rate movements by about a month.

Another factor which might be expected to have an influence is the level of UK interest rates compared with those of other countries. The graph at the bottom of Figure 24.2 shows the pattern of UK interest rates relative to those in the US, taking into account any forward discounts or premiums in the currencies. The shape of this graph is, of course, similar to that which would be obtained by differencing the individual charts for the two sets of interest rates given in Figure 22.6. A higher relative UK interest rate might be expected to produce a higher relative exchange rate. In fact, cause and effect appear to be just the opposite of what might have been expected: it seems more likely, from the graphs, that UK interest rates tend to rise late in the year as a *consequence* of a declining exchange rate, and in an attempt to counteract that decline.

Two other factors which might affect exchange rates are the level of UK reserves and, of course, the price of oil.

We know that there is a *long-term* correlation between oil prices and the value of the pound; as a result, the pound rose strongly in parallel with oil prices in 1979 and 1980. However, no such clear relationship exists between the purely *seasonal* variations in oil prices and exchange rates. We saw the seasonal pattern in the spot price of North Sea oil in Chapter 21 (Figure 21.2). The pound has tended to follow oil prices in the first half of the year, but not in the second half: as oil prices have risen in anticipation of the winter, the pound has been at its *lowest* ebb. At that time of the year, the positive effect of the stronger oil price was outweighed by the deterioration in other components of the terms of trade.

The UK's official reserves do not show any significant seasonal variation, so far as I can detect. I used 1979–84 data, corrected so as to eliminate the effects of the revaluation which takes place each March.

So, to sum up as far as the 'trade-weighted' index is concerned: (a) there is a significant seasonal pattern; (b) it closely follows the pattern in our terms of trade with other countries; (c) neither oil prices (surprisingly) nor our reserves can account for much of the seasonal pattern; (d) an interest rate differential between the UK and the US seems to be *caused* by exchange rate changes, rather than vice versa.

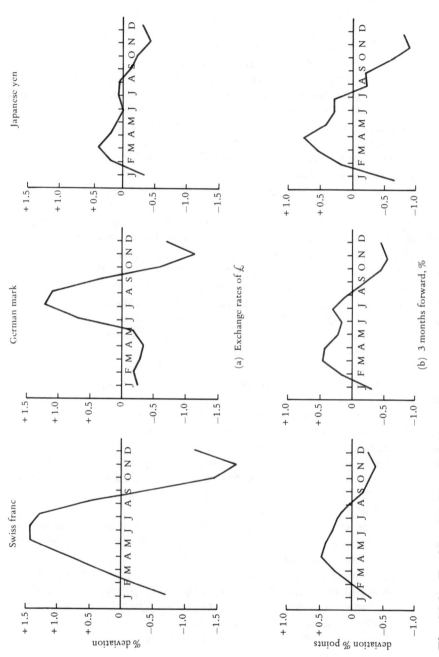

(a) Exchange rates of £

(b) 3 months forward, %

Fig. 24.3 Exchange rates against strong currencies

166

The pound v. the dollar

There was no significant or systematic relationship between the pound and the dollar, with the exception that the pound tended to be strong in January and February. The dollar accounts for a considerable proportion of the 'trade-weighted index'; it looks as if it is the strength of the pound against the dollar (or, conversely, a weak dollar) which is largely responsible for the strong start to the year for the trade-weighted index.

You will recall that we saw a practical consequence of this effect in Chapter 20. Commodity prices are normally quoted in dollars. At the turn of the year, purchasers of commodities in sterling have benefited from the relative strength of the pound at that time.

Other 'strong' currencies

Figure 24.3 summarizes the results for the 'strong' currencies, namely the Swiss franc, the German mark and the Japanese yen. It is seasonal strength against these currencies which mainly accounts for the overall strength of the pound (as measured by its trade-weighted index) in the months May to August. The seasonal *weakness* in the pound against most currencies, from September to the end of the year, is the most consistent feature of the whole analysis.

The same diagram shows what appear to be intriguing similarities between the actual exchange rate factors for each month and those for the 3-month forward margins. In markets with perfect foresight, the peak in the 3-month margin might be expected to occur three months earlier than the peak in the 'spot' exchange rate. However, the graphs suggest that the market's view of the future is that it will not be appreciably different from today. I'm not entirely surprised at this result; I suspect that it applies to a wide range of factors, not just exchange rates. (Stephen Marris, in *Deficits and the Dollar: The world at risk*, makes some pertinent observations on this subject (pp.117–22). He concludes that: 'the majority of operators in the exchange markets are concentrating on what is likely to happen in the next few hours or days rather than the next months or years.')

Ostensibly, this observation should give the astute financial trader the opportunity to 'beat the market'. However, before you rush off to try your hand (or your money), I must issue two warnings.

Firstly, the seasonal effects are fairly small. The difference between the seasonal peak and the seasonal trough is in the range 1 per cent to 3 per cent, depending on the currency; such small changes would be easily swamped by secular movements in exchange rates which, in any one year, might be ten times that amount.

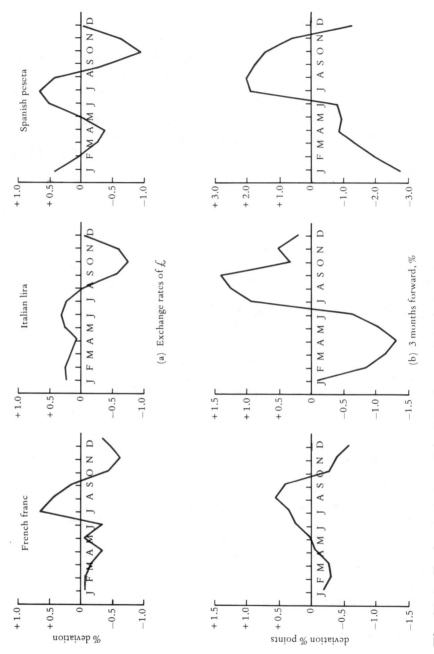

Fig. 24.4 Exchange rates against weaker currencies

168

Secondly, the seasonal factors are not very consistent from one year to another. In fact, for 1985 – the year immediately following those which were analysed – the pound hit an all-time *low* against the dollar in the January/February period. The year-end minimum is a consistent feature when comparing the pound against various other currencies, but not all that consistent when comparing one year with another. The most consistent year-to-year feature in the whole analysis was the *relative* strength of the pound against the Swiss franc in May/June.

So, if you are thinking of opening a Swiss bank account (and why not?), then it looks as though you would do slightly better to convert your pounds to francs in the middle of the year.

'Weak' currencies

The results for the French franc, Italian lira and Spanish peseta are shown in Figure 24.4. The exchange rates follow broadly the pattern of the trade-weighted index.

I had thought that the peseta might be seasonally strong (i.e. the pound against the peseta seasonally weak) in the period June to August, reflecting a demand for Spanish currency by holidaymakers. This is not the case: the seasonal pattern of the pound against the peseta is almost exactly the same as its pattern compared to a basket of currencies. (The 'forward margin' data for the peseta contained a number of 'freak' figures, and I would not put much faith in that particular graph.)

Conclusions

I've looked only at the way in which the pound varies against other currencies. In order to obtain a complete picture of currency movements, it would be necessary to analyse the relationships between each currency and every other one. Combining my own results with what little I have seen reported elsewhere of the dollar's seasonal pattern, we can arrive at some broad generalizations about the chief seasonal strengths and weaknesses of different currencies, as follows:

Jan–Feb $ weak against most other currencies, including the £
Mar–May   neutral
Jun–Aug   £ and $ both strong against most other currencies
Sep–Dec   £ weak against most other currencies

Paradoxically, the most interesting of these periods is perhaps the one in which nothing much is happening, namely March to May. Financial markets supposedly dislike uncertainty and change: by and large, the March–May period is one which produces few major deviations from the long-term trends in exchange rates. It is tempting to think that this is consistent with the general air of confidence which, as we have seen earlier in the book, characterizes that part of the year.

The results for January are worth some further consideration. Whilst seasonality in economic matters generally has tended to be ignored, it *has* recently been quite fashionable to refer to a 'January crisis' for the pound, as if this was a normal occurrence. In fact, it is a quite recent phenomenon, which can be traced to a combination of the falling trend in oil prices (see Chapter 20 on Commodities) and the consequential effects of major public share offers (see Chapter 27). Once oil prices have settled down and the privatization programme is largely completed, then it would be reasonable to expect the seasonal pattern to return to the one illustrated in this chapter; in other words, for January to become, once again, a relatively *good* month for the pound.

25 Gold

Officially, the role of gold has lost its dominance as a reserve currency; unofficially it is still one of the first beneficiaries of any concern over the state of the world's economic or political situation. This inverse relationship between the gold price and confidence is graphically illustrated in Figure 25.1.

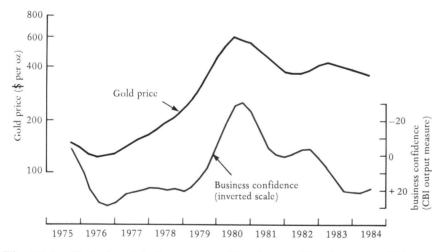

Fig. 25.1 Relationship between gold price and business confidence

It might be expected, therefore, that the same inverse relationship would hold true on a month-to-month basis. It is *partially* true, but by no means completely so. Figure 25.2 shows the seasonal pattern of the London gold price. In winter and spring the pattern closely follows a path which *is* the inverse of the confidence graph, e.g. low in March and April when confidence is high. However, in June and July it does *not* mirror the subsequent decline in business confidence; on the contrary, the gold price is just as weak as other factors – not only business confidence, but also UK stock and bond prices. I have no explanation for this observation; it is too pronounced to be a statistical freak. This is a further example of a general phenomenon which we have come across before in this book: namely, relationships between series of data which are known to exist in the long term often break down (or even go into reverse) when we look at the seasonal patterns.

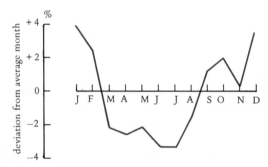

Fig. 25.2   Price of gold ($ per oz.)

Another relationship we might expect to observe would be one between the price of gold and the value of shares traded on the Johannesburg stock exchange. Figure 25.3 shows the seasonal pattern for the *Rand Daily Mail* Share Index. It *does* appear to follow, reasonably well, the gold price pattern.

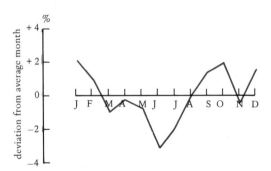

Fig. 25.3   South African share prices (Rand Daily Mail Index)

It doesn't follow the gold price exactly, so I thought that it might be interesting to calculate the residual seasonal pattern in the share prices, i.e. the variation which is not explained by the gold price. What I've done in Figure 25.4 is to plot the difference between the two seasonal patterns. The results are intriguing: this residual effect is remarkably like our familiar 'M' pattern. In other words, the South African share price pattern acts as if it comprises two components, one similar to the gold price and one similar to the 'M' factor. (This conclusion is not altered if we displace the scale so as to start in June, as we have done with another southern hemisphere country, Australia).

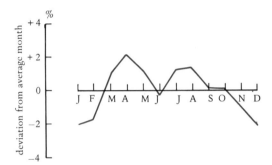

**Fig. 25.4   Difference in seasonal patterns: South African share
prices minus gold price**

Now, I have to say that this kind of analysis needs to be taken with a very large pinch of salt. The two individual series, gold and shares, produce patterns which are inevitably subject to a certain degree of error; the difference between the two is subject to an even higher error. So don't take Figure 25.4 too seriously, but I thought that you might find it interesting.

26 Government finance and money supply

The growth of the public sector has inevitably had an increasing influence on the seasonal patterns of the nation's finances. Both revenue and expenditure have significant seasonal effects; the shortfall of revenue over expenditure –the 'borrowing requirement' – has an even more pronounced effect.

One of the most important events in the nation's financial calendar is the Budget, presented in the spring. It is argued, in this chapter, that the timing of this Budget is a direct cause of some of the instabilities which occur in the economy.

Finally in this chapter we shall look at various measures of money supply which the government uses to target, measure or control the level of activity in the economy.

Government income and expenditure

The aggregate seasonal patterns are shown in Figure 26.1 for total revenue, total expenditure and the central government borrowing requirement.

Revenue is especially high in January, with substantial tax payments falling due in that month. With expenditure being little above average, there is a very pronounced dip in the borrowing needs of central government: in fact, the seasonal deviation for January (and February) is lower even than minus 100 per cent, indicating that central government is a net *repayer* of debt at that time. The magnitude of the tax effect is shown in Figure 26.2. A characteristic of some other forms of government revenue is a strong quarterly pattern – see Figure 26.3 for the seasonal variations in customs and excise duties.

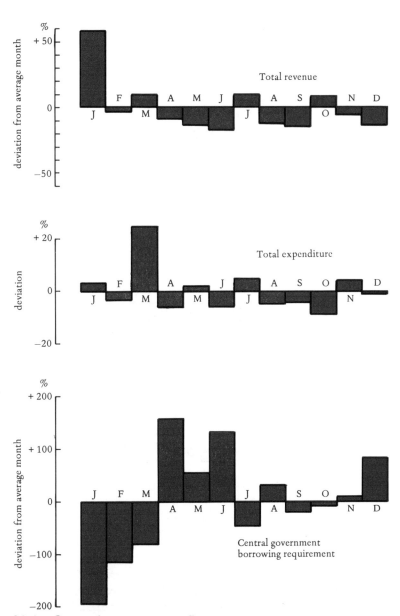

Fig. 26.1   **Central government finances**

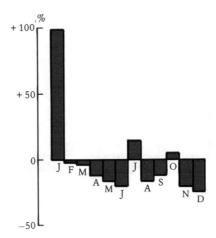

Fig. 26.2   Inland Revenue receipts

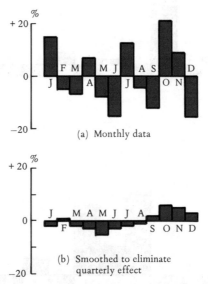

Fig. 26.3   Customs and Excise receipts

Total expenditure (back to Figure 26.1) rises to a sharp seasonal peak in March, as Budget allocations are spent before the end of the financial year. Revenue, also, is quite buoyant in March. Subsequently, a seasonal fall in revenue leads to a substantial borrowing need from April to June.

The significant variations in central government borrowing in the first half of the year do *not* result in corresponding changes in interest rates. Indeed, the actual effect is just the opposite of what we might expect. (If you look back at Figure 22.2, remember that the interest rate patterns are plotted upside down; in other words, the spring peak represents a seasonal *minimum* in interest rates, just when the central government borrowing requirement is reaching its peak.)

Other specific items of government revenue have been pictured earlier in the book:

- duties on beer, wines and spirits (Figure 10.6)
- revenue from vehicle excise duties (Figure 11.1)
- revenue from broadcasting receiving licences (Figure 12.2)
- betting and gaming duties (Figure 12.3).

The Budget

It must be a good thing to make longer-term investment plans in a mood of optimism, and current spending plans in a mood of caution. That is the way to combine growth with a good return on investment.

Hence, it is a good thing for businessmen to do their forward investment planning when optimism reaches its seasonal peak in March and April. On the other hand, this must be exactly the *worst* time for the Chancellor to present the nation's Budget, for current spending and for taxation, for the following 12 months.

A Budget presented in March is almost inevitably going to be based on an over-optimistic view of the year ahead. How often, over the years, have we found that the Budget has been overtaken by events within a matter of months? So often, it seems to have been followed by a 'July package' or an 'autumn package' or something similar.

This is nothing new. A view of UK financial history by stockbrokers de Zoete & Bevan contained the following reference to 1949:

> In September, the pound was devalued from \$4.03 to \$2.80 followed by crisis measures in what was becoming almost a traditional Autumn crisis budget.

You will, I'm sure, immediately connect this comment with the earlier history (Chapter 23) of autumnal pressures on the money markets.

More recently, the year 1976 was a classic example. After an expansionary Budget in the spring, already by July there was a need for cuts of \$1 bn in government spending; by November, the Chancellor was rushing off to the IMF to borrow nearly \$4 bn!

In recent years, in addition to the spring Budget, we have had an Autumn Statement from the Chancellor in November. In the light of what you have read in this book, you might well expect that this Statement would be less optimistic than the subsequent spring Budget. And, indeed, you would be right. The Autumn Statement in 1983 projected tax *increases* for the following financial year; by the time the spring Budget arrived, this had become a *cut* in taxes of nearly £2 bn!

This Autumn Statement, insofar as it sets out some of the longer-term plans and projections which provide the background to the Budget, might actually benefit by being made in a more optimistic season – just as businessmen can benefit by making their future investment plans in the spring.

The government should seriously consider changing the timing of its annual planning and budgeting cycle. Specifically, *the 'Autumn Statement' should be presented in the spring* (and concentrate on longer-term, especially infrastructure proposals); and *the 'Spring Budget' should be presented in the autumn* (and combine both spending and revenue plans for the following year).

I firmly believe that this change would introduce a combination of long-term confidence for investment, short-term spending caution and a much greater degree of stability in financial policies, which would lead to a really significant improvement in the UK's economic performance.

Money supply

The government's macro-economic policies in recent years have been dominated by attempts to control the supply of money. In this way, it has been hoped to achieve reasonable economic growth, whilst controlling inflation. Whilst monetary *targets* have become a feature of economic policy, actually keeping the supply of money within these targets has proved to be more easily said than done. Indeed, so unsuccessful have been these attempts that the importance of money supply numbers has been increasingly pushed into the background.

There are so many of these measures that I ought to start with a brief summary of what some of them mean. The one that is self-explanatory is 'notes and coins in circulation with the public'. We shall see the seasonal pattern for this factor in Figure 26.7a. There is a peak in December to finance Christmas spending; this is then unwound in January. The only other noticeable feature is another peak in July, i.e. at the onset of the main holiday period.

The other more common measures of money supply are:

M0   This is mainly notes and coins in circulation with the public, but also

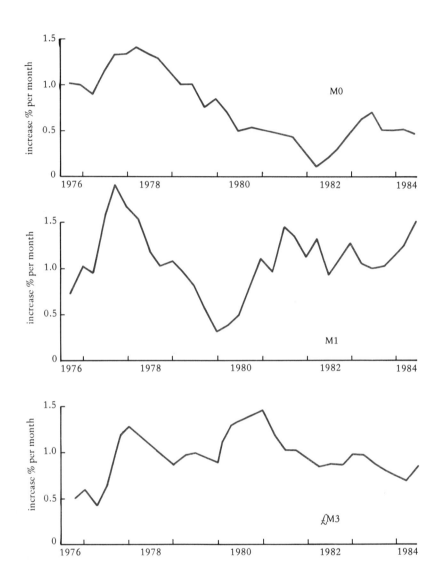

Fig. 26.4   Trends in monetary aggregates

includes such currency held by banks. I actually analysed just the data for notes and coins in circulation, but designate some of the results as 'M0'.

M1   Is a slightly wider measure of 'liquid' assets; as well as actual physical money, it includes bank current accounts which can be drawn upon without notice; also any other assets that can be immediately turned into cash. It does include some interest-bearing deposits, but not a high proportion of the total.

M2   Is no longer used.

M3   Is a 'wide' measure of money supply; it additionally includes bank deposits which earn interest (and which normally, in principle, cannot be withdrawn on demand).

£M3   ('Sterling M3') also includes deposits held overseas.

PSL2 (which is not analysed in this chapter) additionally includes investments such as building society deposits and National Savings.

Before we look in detail at the seasonal pattern, it is instructive to consider longer-term trends. These trends – for M0, M1 and £M3 – are shown in Figure 26.4. There is no obvious similarity between the diagrams; this is surprising for two reasons:

(a)   a substantial component of M1 (normally about one-third) is M0; and a substantial component of £M3 (nearly one half) is M1;

(b)   the government sets different target ranges for the various measures, but those targets are adjusted up or down in tandem, as if the various measures themselves went hand in hand in some way.

More insight can be gained by plotting, not M1 (including, as it does, M0) and £M3 (which includes M1), but the *differences* M1 – M0 and M3 – M1. The results of this analysis are shown in Figure 26.5.

When plotted in this way, it is clear that M1 – M0 and M3 – M1, far from moving in parallel, tend to be *mirror images* of each other. The main reason is also clear from the diagrams, on which I have superimposed the trend in interest rates. (This trend is based on 3-month Treasury Bills; the scale is omitted: it varied between 6 per cent and 16 per cent over the period.) As interest rates rise, there is a natural tendency to prefer interest-bearing securities, and this is borne out by the diagram. When we come to look at the seasonal patterns, we shall therefore look out for any similarity between those for interest rates and £M3 – M1.

In the meantime, we shall look briefly at two other questions concerning the monetary trends: (a) do they anticipate changes in inflation? and (b) do they anticipate changes in real economic activity?

It is often suggested that changes in money supply lead changes in inflation

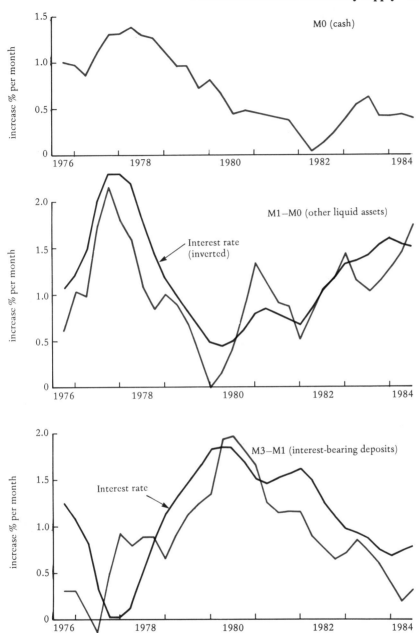

Fig. 26.5   Trends in components of monetary aggregates

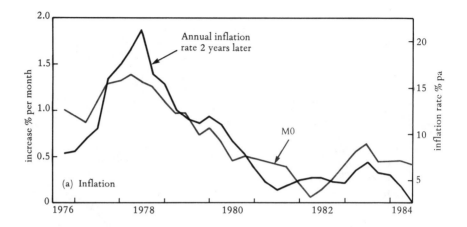

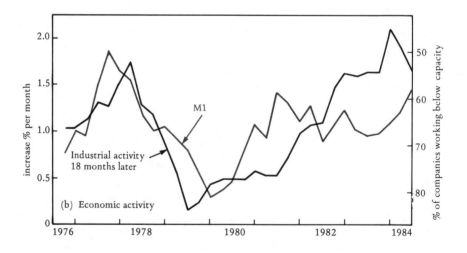

Fig. 26.6   Possible predictive effects of monetary aggregates

by about two years. Such an effect is, indeed, clearly shown in Figure 26.6a. The annual change in the retail price index has followed changes in M0 with a lag of two years. It does not follow any of the other measures pictured in Figures 26.4 and 26.5.

As a measure of economic activity, I have taken the percentage of firms

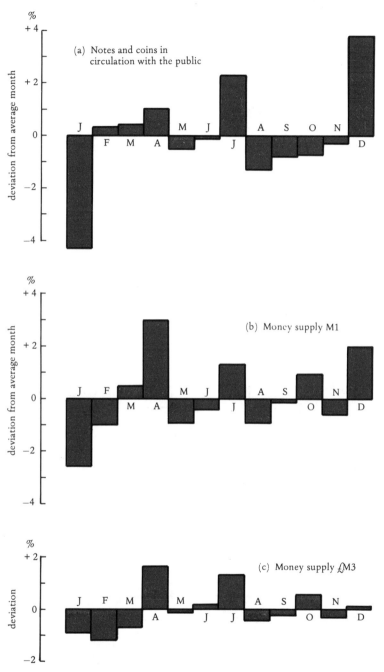

Fig. 26.7   Money supply – monthly changes

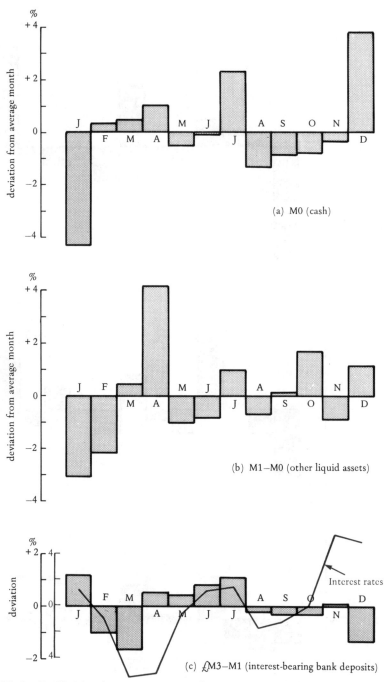

(a) M0 (cash)

(b) M1–M0 (other liquid assets)

Interest rates

(c) £M3–M1 (interest-bearing bank deposits)

Fig. 26.8   Individual components of money supply changes

reporting that they are working below capacity. The substantial fall in activity in 1980/1 was best predicted (with a lead of about 18 months) by the changes in M1 (Figure 26.6b). However, M1 on its own would not have been a very good lead indicator of subsequent economic activity. ('Real' M1, i.e. M1 minus the rate of inflation at the time, would have been much better.)

Because of the long time delays involved in these relationships–two years and eighteen months respectively–it is unlikely that they will give any clues to the factors affecting the seasonal variations in the monetary aggregates.

These seasonal patterns are shown in Figures 26.7 and 26.8. I have used the same procedure as with the long-term trends: in other words, as well as showing M0, M1 and £M3, I have illustrated the patterns for M1 – M0 and £M3 – M1.

I have already referred to one of the most obvious features, namely the large increase in cash in December (which is promptly unwound in January). The Christmas effect is also evident in the £M3 – M1 pattern. We anticipated, from the long-term trend, that this pattern might be affected by interest rate changes. It appears from Figure 26.8c that this is, to some extent, true in the short term as well as in the longer term. With the main exception of the period leading up to Christmas, there is a tendency for the level of interest-bearing deposits to increase as interest rates increase. (Note that, in this case, the interest rate pattern – for 3-month Treasury Bills – is *not* inverted.)

The one other feature of the seasonal pattern is the strong movement of money out of long-term deposits into 'sight' deposits in April (and, to a much lesser extent, in October).

With that brief look at government finance, we have come to the end of the analysis of historical data. In the next section of the book, I shall attempt to pull together some of the threads which have emerged in our wide-ranging analysis which has covered (albeit briefly) very many aspects of life. Just before doing so, I shall bring the historical results further up to date by reviewing some of the data for 1985 and 1986.

Part IV
SUMMARY

27 Is the past a good guide to forecasting the future?

In Parts II and III we looked at the historical evidence of seasonality in a wide range of data series. The question we shall consider now is: Can these same patterns be used as a good guide to seasonal variations in the future?

We can anticipate, in advance, that some patterns will be highly repeatable and others less so. There are two ways of distinguishing the one group from the other.

The first method is to look at the computer print-outs and study the historical year-to-year repeatability of the seasonal factors for each month. If, for the 10 years' data which we have normally analysed, these historical monthly factors are very consistent from one year to another, then it is a reasonable assumption that a similar pattern of seasonal factors can be projected into the future (within predictable confidence limits).

Whilst this is generally true, it is always best to be cautious about such an approach. It is common to find, with any statistical forecasting system, that the future falls all too often outside its predicted range of probability. Entirely new influences can arise which do not affect the historical data. For instance, the amount of cash held by individuals has been strongly affected by the rapid growth in credit cards. Money supply data from earlier years *may* not be a reliable guide to events in the 'plastics age'.

Personally, I always prefer to test the forecasting ability of any equation (or pattern) by comparing it with *new* data, *outside* the time frame which has been analysed.

Both methods will be used in this chapter, in order to indicate the predictive value of the various seasonal patterns.

Most of the patterns which have been illustrated were based on data for the decade 1975–84. The most obvious approach, therefore, is to see what

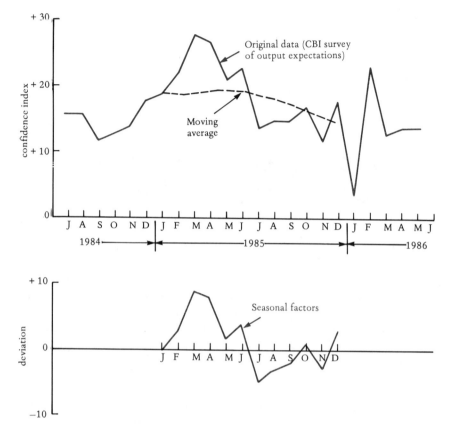

Fig. 27.1   Calculating the actual seasonal factors for 1985

actually happened in 1985 (and 1986). It's actually not quite as straightforward as that, as you may recognize from the way in which the seasonal factors are calculated.

These seasonal factors represent the deviations from the moving averages of the monthly data (i.e. from the underlying trend/cycle, with any purely seasonal effect first removed). So, it is not going to be enough just to look at the actual 1985 data; we need to see how the individual 1985 monthly figures differ from their moving averages. In order to calculate these moving averages, we actually need to look at the data from July 1984 to June 1986 – a period of *two* years. This is what has been done to produce the charts shown in this chapter.

An example of the calculation is shown in Figure 27.1, taking the example of UK business confidence. By now, this diagram will be self-explanatory.

You will notice, in particular, that the very low actual figure for November is not quite so low when measured as a deviation from its moving average: July can now be seen to have included a stronger negative seasonal impact in 1985 than did November, because it occurred against a background of generally greater optimism.

The plot of the original data also illustrates why it is really necessary to calculate seasonal factors averaged over several years. One year's data can be quite erratic. The upward jump in December 1985 is the only part of the seasonal pattern which differs radically from the average pattern shown in Figure 16.1; it can be seen, in Figure 27.1, that the series seems to have become generally rather erratic around (and just after) that time.

We shall now move on to consider the actual outcome, beyond December 1984, for many of the individual series which have been described in earlier chapters.

It is actually quite easy to summarize the 1985 results for those series illustrated in Part II, by saying that almost all of them followed the average pattern rather closely.

This was to be expected for the 'social' factors: the seasonal factors calculated earlier were generally very consistent from year to year. As usual, in 1985 people tended to be born in the spring and early summer, to be married in late summer, to be divorced in the last quarter and to die in mid-winter. They were most confident but least healthy in March; they went on holiday, bought cars, went to the cinema and generally started to become more aggressive in August; and they had their usual spending spree in December. (Oddly, they also went to the cinema more often than usual in December.)

Some of the 'everyday life' factors of most interest to businessmen are illustrated in Figures 27.2 to 27.4.

The employment-related diagrams shown in Figure 27.2 generally follow the earlier patterns very closely. Two differences which are evident are, in fact, continuations of trends which actually started a few years earlier:

- the seasonal peak in unfilled vacancies (in October) has been as high as the June peak since 1983;
- the low unemployment figure for August has been a feature since 1981.

The sharp increase in average earnings in March 1985 shows the effect of the ending of the year-long miner's strike.

Retail prices and sales (Figure 27.3) also conform closely to the patterns established earlier – sales more so than prices. Missing in 1985 was the upward blip in non-food prices in July.

The measures of building society finances shown in Figures 27.4a and c are remarkably similar to the earlier averages – much more so than one might reasonably expect in the case of such a variable factor as the net increase in

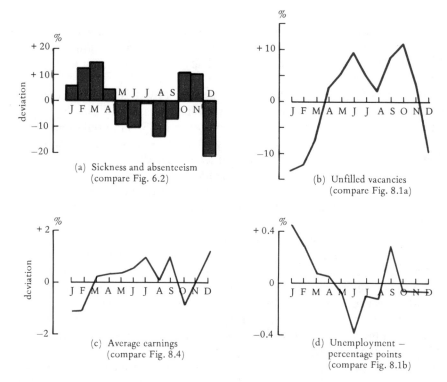

(a) Sickness and absenteeism
(compare Fig. 6.2)

(b) Unfilled vacancies
(compare Fig. 8.1a)

(c) Average earnings
(compare Fig. 8.4)

(d) Unemployment –
percentage points
(compare Fig. 8.1b)

Fig. 27.2   Employment

money invested in the societies.

It is only when we come to house prices that we encounter the first real surprise (and, indeed, the *only* really significant variation from the patterns illustrated in Part II). The fall in prices in mid-summer (relative to a continuing upward trend) was most unexpected. To put this into perspective, it should be mentioned that the pattern given earlier, in Figure 13.3c, was one of the least statistically significant of all those given in that section, so perhaps it should not have been quite such a surprise. There is, in fact, a possible logical explanation for the unusual pattern; as discussed later, it can be related (surprisingly, perhaps) to the British Telecom share flotation in late 1984. Subsequently, in 1986, house prices had returned to a more normal pattern – moving ahead strongly in mid-summer.

Turning now to comparisons with the patterns given in Part III, we start by looking at indices of business confidence in various countries. We have already seen a UK index (CBI output series) in the introductory illustration, Figure 27.1. This chart is repeated in Figure 27.5, along with the patterns for the EEC in total, for Italy, and for the United States.

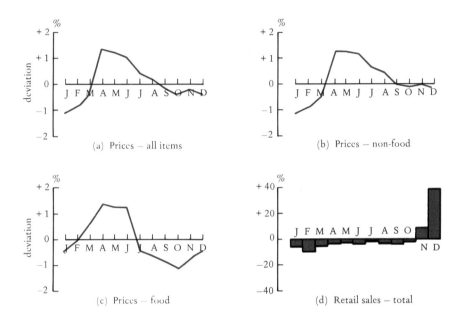

Fig. 27.3   **Retail prices and sales (compare Figs. 9.2 and 10.2)**

All of these 1985 patterns conform remarkably closely with their longer-term averages. It is not just the general shapes which are similar, but also the magnitudes of the seasonal variations. The one slight exception is the positive deviation in December with the CBI series. We have already seen how this series was rather erratic at that time. The total EEC series – even for one year – tends to average out such erratic movements in the data for any one country, and so is less susceptible to the occasional 'freak' result.

In the light of these results, there can be no reasonable doubt that the analysis given in Chapter 16 has uncovered a pronounced, persistent and important factor in business behaviour.

The earlier stock market patterns may well have been of especial interest to a wide range of readers. So, did 1985 turn out as expected?

Figure 27.6a was typical of all classes of shares in that year. Two months in particular are out of line: in both January and November share prices were higher than we might have anticipated. This is reflected exactly in the patterns of share transactions: unusually high numbers of transactions in both January and November corresponded to the high share prices at those times.

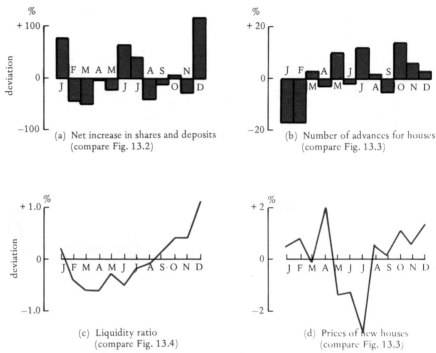

(a) Net increase in shares and deposits
(compare Fig. 13.2)

(b) Number of advances for houses
(compare Fig. 13.3)

(c) Liquidity ratio
(compare Fig. 13.4)

(d) Prices of new houses
(compare Fig. 13.3)

Fig. 27.4   Building societies and housing

In Figure 27.6b, the January transactions figure has been distinguished from the other months, because it was a very artificial figure: it was grossly distorted by the aftermath of the huge British Telecom share flotation in November of the previous year. (Dealings began in December 1984, and total share transactions in that month were double what they would otherwise have been. In order not to distort all of the subsequent moving averages, the actual figure was replaced, in the calculations, by a more normal average figure.) That flotation had a substantial, one-off effect in inflating both transactions and share prices at that time. Moving forwards to 1986, the 'normal' pattern returned with a vengeance: the stock market peak of early April (and the subsequent sharp decline) was a dramatic example of the underlying seasonal forces which affect share prices.

The 'British Telecom effect' – which stimulated interest in (and prices of) shares a few months earlier than usual – can also be seen in the pattern of new share issues, which peaked two months early. As usual, a stock market boom stimulated companies to go to the market to raise additional equity finance,

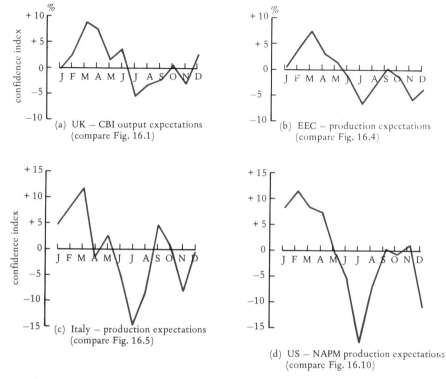

(a) UK – CBI output expectations
(compare Fig. 16.1)

(b) EEC – production expectations
(compare Fig. 16.4)

(c) Italy – production expectations
(compare Fig. 16.5)

(d) US – NAPM production expectations
(compare Fig. 16.10)

Fig. 27.5   Business confidence

after the inevitable time delay to organize the issue. In 1986, the new issues 'boom' was back to a more normal June peak.

The mini-boom in share prices and activity in November 1985 coincided with one of those periodic bouts of 'merger mania' which affect companies which have more money than good ideas and which tend to come grinding to a halt after the spring peak in the stock market.

We saw, in Chapter 17, that the Italian stock market has one of the most pronounced seasonal behaviour patterns. With no 'British Telecom effect' to distort it, the Milan index followed its average path fairly closely: the only notable difference was that the mid-year trough occurred a little early. The pronounced seasonality of the Italian market was in evidence again later, with the very sharp fall of around 30 per cent in a month, starting in May 1986.

The *Economist* commodity price patterns in Chapter 20 had a quite low level of statistical significance. The patterns were by no means consistent from one year to another. Nevertheless, 1985 turned out to be quite a normal

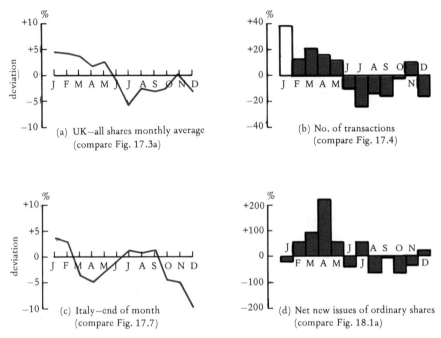

Fig. 27.6   **The stock market**

year for dollar prices (see Figure 27.7). The one exception was that metals prices did not exhibit a secondary peak in the autumn.

Two seasonal patterns were given in Figure 21.2 for oil prices. Coincidentally, the actual behaviour in 1985 and 1986 followed each of the two patterns in turn: 1985 reflected the pattern for 'US prices at wells'; the dramatic changes in the following year were an exaggerated reflection of the pattern for North Sea 'spot' prices.

It is appropriate to concentrate on dollar indices of commodities, since commodities are generally priced in that currency. The sterling indices (not illustrated) were distorted by the slightly unusual pattern for the sterling exchange rate, illustrated in Figure 27.8. The pound was unusually weak at the beginning of the year; in fact, it fell to its then all-time low. Subsequently, following a sharp increase in interest rates, it recovered to follow its more normal pattern, reaching its peak on schedule in July.

The exchange rate against the Swiss franc was more or less as expected; the '3-month forward margin' was – as we found earlier – a reflection more of the

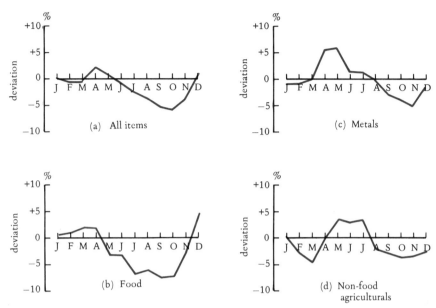

Fig. 27.7   Commodities — dollar prices (compare Fig. 20.1)

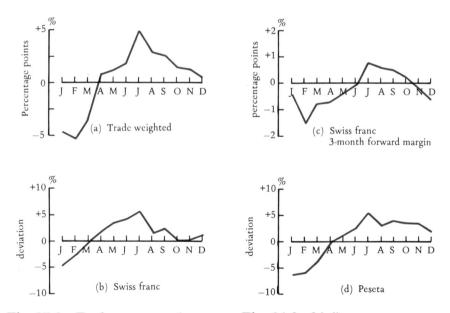

Fig. 27.8   Exchange rates (compare Figs 24.2 – 24.4)

immediate situation than of that which actually occurred three months later.

Notice that, when looking at a single year in isolation, the magnitudes of these variations are substantially higher than for the long-run averages. There is considerable year-to-year variation in these exchange rate patterns, and therefore the averaging process inevitably damps down the amplitude of any individual year's variability.

The weakness of sterling in early 1985 was not a reflection of any large, coincident increase in money supply. The money supply patterns shown in Figure 27.9 are very similar to their longer-term averages. M1 and £M3 went a little haywire in June and July (for a reason which we shall see later); otherwise, the patterns are remarkably similar for measures which are usually regarded as being very erratic at the best of times (most especially in January, when tax payments fall due).

In fact, the weakness of sterling in early 1985 can be more easily understood as a response to a surge in M1 and £M3 in November of the previous year. Interest rates then fell and money supply rose sharply, very much against the seasonal trend. This was almost certainly connected with the attempts to ensure the success of the massive British Telecom share offer to the public. The unseasonal element of the money supply rise, namely about £2 bn, was similar to the amount of money raised from the private sector at that time. This estimate also fits in very well with a press comment on the BT share offer: 'The Bank of England made "temporary facilities" of up to £1.5 bn available to the banking system to relieve anticipated money market liquidity shortages.' (*Financial Times*, 28 November 1984, page 1.) It is logical to assume, also, that the large unseasonal rise in M1 in June 1985 was connected with the second instalment payment for BT shares; in this case, however, the effect was immediately unwound in July. Perhaps, one day, someone may calculate just how much of the benefit to the UK economy of the British Telecom flotation was dissipated in the consequential effects of an inflated money supply, a weaker pound, and the subsequent need to push up interest rates to 'crisis' levels.

In Figure 27.10 this large, unseasonal rise in interest rates in February is described as 'unexpected'. It *was* unexpected in the sense that it was unusual compared with earlier years; however, it is much more understandable in terms of the corrective action necessary in response to earlier unseasonal policy decisions. (This large unseasonal rise in interest rates would, incidentally, also explain the strange subsequent behaviour of house prices.)

What we have seen, in this chapter, is that the seasonal patterns of earlier years have generally been rather well reproduced subsequently. Inevitably, there are random, unpredictable events and effects which mean that any one year's patterns have their individual characteristics. However, what we have also seen is that the distortions in seasonal economic patterns can be caused, not just by genuinely random effects, but even more so by important, specific

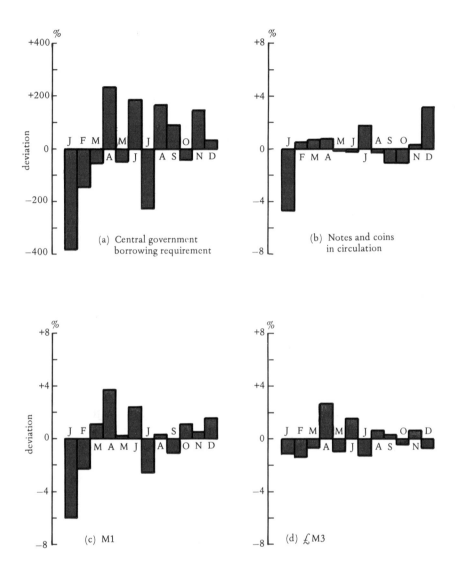

Fig. 27.9 Government finance and money supply (compare Figs. 26.1 and 26.7)

policy decisions. (The gold price weakness early in 1985 − see Figure 27.10b − was a reflection of the equally unseasonal strength of the dollar, although that in turn cannot be related so easily to any single policy decision.)

There were not all that many 'distortions' in 1985; many − indeed, almost all − of these that we have seen for the UK can be explained as a

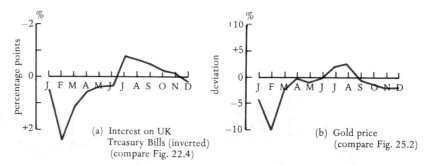

Fig. 27.10   **Two unexpected results**

consequence of the British Telecom share flotation. I am convinced that it would have been infinitely better to have sold those shares to the public in March or April – months in which the public's appetite for shares would not have needed to have been artificially stimulated anything like as much as in November. It was the advertising stimulus, rather than the disappointing public response, which remains the most memorable feature of the British Gas share flotation in November 1986. The smaller TSB share offer in the previous month must be rated a success: even in October, the British public know when they are getting a real bargain!

This discussion leads naturally on to the subject of politics, and the answer to the question you were left with in Chapter 2. You will recall that you were asked to consider when the UK Conservative party would be likely to perform best in a General Election. Before giving you my results, I ought to emphasize a particular difficulty with this analysis: it was not possible to obtain a consistent long-term set of data on public opinion, for the following reasons:

(a)   Public opinion polls on voting intentions were not carried out every month until fairly recently (I am indebted to MORI for historical data on voting intentions);

(b)   Changes of government confuse the picture: is a particular seasonal effect a reflection of the standing of a particular party, or of whichever party happens to be in power at the time?

(c)   It seemed safest to ignore polls taken in the same month as a General Election.

(d)   A third force in British politics has emerged in recent years.

Nevertheless, a reasonably coherent picture emerges from an analysis of various kinds of survey data (voting intentions; degree of satisfaction with the government). The picture looks like this:

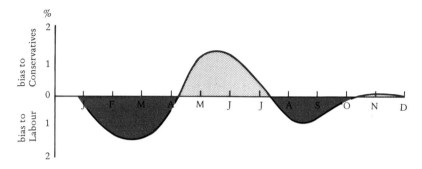

The popularity of the Conservative party is at its seasonal peak in May/June; that of the Labour party in February/March (with a secondary peak in August/September). In recent years, the peak in popularity for the Conservatives has actually tended to be June rather than May.

The full analysis suggests that this kind of pattern is indicative of *party support*, whichever of the two parties happens to be in power at the time; there does not seem to be any particular seasonal bias towards or against the ruling party.

It is interesting to compare this chart with the results of all of the General Elections which have taken place since the immediate postwar election of July 1945. The results correspond astonishingly well to the chart, as follows:

February/March	2 Labour wins (1950, 1966); 1 with no overall majority (1974)
May/June	All 4 won by the Conservatives (1955, 1970, 1979, 1983)
October	2 Labour wins (1964, 1974); 2 Conservative wins (1951, 1959).

No elections were held in any other months.

It will not have escaped your notice that the general shape of the curve (a primary and secondary peak, plus a primary and secondary trough) is yet another example of the M-factor at work.

This chapter has dealt mainly with one particular year, and with the forecasting potential of the various seasonal patterns, M-shaped and otherwise. We shall now (and finally) revert to the average patterns established by studying seasonal behaviour over several years. In the next chapter, the intention is to pull together some of the many threads from which our story has been woven, and to see whether we can draw together some general conclusions.

28   Conclusions

The primary intention of this book has been to present the results rather than to interpret them. Nevertheless, I shall hazard a few general thoughts that have arisen in the course of this work.

As to the results themselves, I trust that you have found them to be interesting and, in several cases, surprising. Even where the seasonal patterns have been much as you might expect, you may have been unaware of just how great (or how small) are the month-to-month variations.

Business decisions

It has been a particular aim to present the results of much original analysis into the seasonal patterns of business confidence. Decisions taken by businessmen have a profound effect on us all, and it is perhaps of some concern to find that there is a certain degree of 'irrationality' in that decision-making process, arising solely from the general state of mind of businessmen according to the time of the year. I hope that the book helps in a practical way to overcome this problem. In particular, when decisions are made at certain times of the year (e.g. decisions to cancel or defer new investments or new projects), perhaps boards of directors might pause for a moment to ensure that they are not just reacting to a natural bout of seasonal pessimism.

The 'M' factor

The book has certainly *not* found a simple answer to the question: why *is* there a significant seasonal pattern in business confidence? This seasonal pattern was seen to be a clear example of what we have termed the monthly 'M' factor: in other words, a pattern shaped roughly like the letter 'M'.

We saw that this same pattern, or something very similar, was present in very many series of data. For instance, in the UK, a very similar pattern was found with interest rates, and it might therefore be concluded that it is the interest rate pattern which causes the changes in business confidence. However, if this were so, then we would expect to find the same relationship with interest rates in North America – which we don't. It seems likely that business confidence (in most countries) *and* interest rates (in the UK) are *both* affected by some third factor, such as the seasonal demand for money. There was some evidence that the supply of money, to match the seasonal patterns of demand, is better managed in the US than in the UK, and this is what causes the seasonal pattern of interest rates in the two countries to differ.

Human behaviour

The analysis of business confidence is just one illustration of a more general observation: namely, that people's opinions about the future are dictated, to a very large extent, by current circumstances. We saw this with exchange rates (comparing current exchange rates with 'forward' rates); also with stocks and shares (buying activity being greatest when share prices reach their seasonal peak). It is psychologically extremely difficult to go in the opposite direction to the herd, but there should be an advantage at the end of the day (or, rather, the year) for those who do.

Long-term v. short-term relationships

We have seen that a number of relationships which we take for granted over the long term break down when we look at a shorter period of time. There are many factors which we assume automatically to be *mirror images* of each other (and which *are* over the longer term), which turn out to be almost *identical* to each other as far as their seasonal patterns are concerned.

A simple example of this was the pattern of short-time and overtime working illustrated in Chapter 8. It is natural to expect short-time working to rise when overtime working falls, and vice versa. This is true when we compare the long-term trends; it is *not* true when we look at variations within a year.

We saw several other examples where the expected 'mirror image' turned out to be no such thing (just the opposite, in fact). Three examples were illustrated in Chapters 13 and 14. Investments of new money in building societies, in unit trusts and in premium bonds are *not* the mirror images of withdrawals. Far from moving in the opposite directions to each other, they tend to go up and down in unison.

In fact, what seems to happen is that both sides of the picture go up and down together, according to fluctuations in the general level of economic activity. At certain times of the year (corresponding to the periods of high business and investor confidence), activity in total increases – both buying *and* selling. At other times of the year principally the Christmas and summer holiday periods – the majority of people have other things on their mind.

Small ripples produce large waves

Small seasonal differences in causal factors can result in large seasonal differences in the consequential effects. We came across an example of this when looking at the months in which companies raise new share capital. The sequence of events goes something like this:

1 Relatively small seasonal changes occur in factors which might affect business opinion – e.g. levels of output, interest rates, share prices, etc.
2 These changes become amplified in the minds of businessmen: they themselves undergo substantially larger changes in their general feeling of optimism or pessimism.
3 These attitudinal changes become amplified even further when it comes to making business decisions: i.e. a modest change in optimism/pessimism can make all the difference between a 'go' and a 'no go' decision.
4 With all businessmen reacting in the same way to the same stimuli, the aggregate effect on the national economy can be very large indeed.

So, what starts out as a small seasonal pattern, with a maximum variation of plus or minus a few per cent, ends up with a pattern of final decisions which might exhibit monthly variations measured in a few *hundreds* of percentage points.

The greatest seasonal effects are at times of rapid change

One of the features of the analysis which I have personally found very surprising is that seasonal patterns are not swamped when large changes take place in the underlying trends. Indeed, the opposite appears to be more frequently the case: seasonal patterns seem to be *more* pronounced at times of rapid change. When a major change occurs – either up or down – it is often the case that the change is largely concentrated in those months in which some corresponding change would be expected on seasonal grounds alone. We saw this effect with both interest rates and business confidence; also, very recently, with the timing of the oil price collapse.

If this conclusion is valid – then the opposite is, of course, also the case. In other words, nothing drastic is likely to occur (from an economic/business point of view) in March and April in particular. Perhaps this is the time when most senior executives should take their holidays! Better still, it is the ideal period in the year to set aside time to consider longer-term plans for the business: such deliberations are unlikely to be distracted by immediate problems, and they will be carried out in a mood of optimism.

In Chapter 26 it was argued that this is precisely the *worst* time for the government to present its annual Budget. The buoyancy which is evident at that time can lead to an over-optimistic view of the economy, and hence of government revenues, and consequently of acceptable government expenditure. All too often, the inevitable outcome has been the later introduction of some measures to compensate (and, maybe, over-compensate) for those over-optimistic Budgets.

The timing of crises and panics

The last two points in this summary, taken together, suggest that crises and panics should be likely to occur only in certain months.

We have seen extensive evidence to indicate that March and April are 'good' months from many points of view. We have seen this in a wide range of factors such as interest rates, share prices and confidence; also in the stability of exchange rates in those months. The suggestion is that there is some deeper, underlying factor which is the ultimate cause; for instance, it is likely that the demands for credit at that time of the year are particularly modest. We have also seen that this effect is nothing new; in some cases, we have traced it back over several decades.

If small changes in the underlying factors can become amplified into very substantial changes in the end results, then we might suppose that financial crises and panics would tend *not* to be triggered when the normal seasonal demand for credit is low, but that they *would* be more likely to be triggered in months when such demand is high.

It would be very interesting if we could test this theory. Luckily, we can.

A history of financial crises has been written by Charles P. Kindleberger, in a book entitled '*Manias, Panics and Crashes*'. He tabulates a long history of such events and identifies the months which witnessed what he categorizes as crises, crashes and panics. There were 16 distinguishable events from 1800 to 1960. When these are plotted out, the result is as shown in the diagram.

I have allocated some of the listed crises between different months to produce the diagram: one of them because it was defined as occurring in 'spring' rather than in a particular month; others because a crisis or related crises affected different countries at different times of the year.

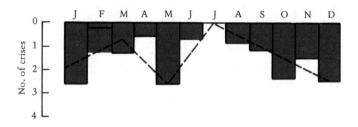

The chart is plotted upside down, in keeping with the general convention used in this book: the occurrence of a crisis is regarded as a negative factor.

Crises and panics are, by their nature, few in number, hence we do not really have a large enough sample to analyse.

Nevertheless, the pattern does seem strikingly similar to our familiar 'M' pattern. The timing of the peaks and troughs is roughly what we would have expected, although perhaps not exactly. The high-risk period from October to January conforms precisely to the period when interest rates are high and confidence in most countries is low. On the other hand, the secondary peak for crises (May) does not coincide exactly with the secondary peak in interest rates (July). July has, in fact, often witnessed 'mini-crises' (at least in the UK), but apparently no 'maxi-crises'. May is the month in which the *rate of increase* of interest rates (and decline of confidence) are particularly high.

My first reaction on seeing the shape of this chart was 'eureka!' Taken in conjunction with the other examples of the 'M' factor, it seemed that here was an original contribution to anticipating the timing of financial crises. This sense of discovery was short-lived, as I then came across the following comment by an American author:

Is there any tendency for financial panics to occur in those seasons of the year when the money market is normally stringent? To this question, the evidence points strongly to an affirmative answer. Of the eight panics which have occurred since '. . .', four took place in the fall or early winter, three broke out in May and one extended from March until well along in November. . . .

Here is another illustration of the old principle that a chain will break at its weakest link.

The conclusions are, as you can see, exactly in line with those which I have illustrated above. The remarkable thing is not just the extent of the agreement, but that the comments are from a paper written as long ago as 1911! (It was by E. W. Kemmerer, based on panics occurring between 1873 and 1907; you may remember that I referred to his work in the history of interest rate analyses.)

I can only hope that my own conclusions look equally relevant in 75 years' time!

In order to bring the analysis up to date, it is worth noting the timing of the most recent financial crises, namely:

- UK stock market crash and secondary banking crisis – November/December 1973; final panic selling – November/December 1974
- Mexico's debt moratorium – August 1982
- Rescue of Continental Illinois Bank – May 1984.

Again, these dates fit very well with the picture which we have just seen.

The paper by J. A. Miron, referred to in Chapter 23, also looks at the incidence of financial panics around the turn of the century and up to (and just after) the Wall Street crash of October 1929. In the other paper which I mentioned in Chapter 23 (that by T. A. Clark), the author mentions that he intends to report his own findings on the connection between interest rate seasonals and financial panics. I wonder whether this sudden surge of interest is an omen of something to come?!

Seasonal pattern 'finger prints'

The calculation of seasonal patterns could be a useful tool in deciding whether two series of data are related to each other in some way (or each related to some third factor). A particular example of such a 'finger print' was given very early in the book, in Chapter 5. We saw that the seasonal pattern of deaths due to the 'cot syndrome' was precisely in line with that for natural causes of death, and quite different from man-inflicted causes. There must be many situations in which the comparison of seasonal patterns could help to resolve an argument between conflicting theories.

The general importance of seasonal adjustments

In fulfilling the main objective of the book – namely to describe the patterns of seasonal variations – I have tried also to emphasize how important it is to take seasonal factors into account. Very many of the published economic series of data which we use are already seasonally adjusted for us. However, other published series are not, and probably most people and companies do not seasonally adjust their own data. For almost any application which I can think of in business, it is really better to work with seasonally adjusted figures.

Seasonal patterns and long-term cycles

I have personally found that most of the changes which occur in economic life are better understood if related to *three* kinds of cyclical phenomena:

● seasonal changes
● the business cycle
● a 'long-wave' economic cycle

Several other cycles have been distinguished and described by other people, but usually the three listed above are the critical ones. In recent years, it has been fashionable to concentrate on the ups and downs of the business cycle. This has a period which varies considerably, but is usually around 4 or 5 years from peak to peak (or trough to trough).

The long-wave cycle is even more indeterminate; indeed, many (if not most) economists would dispute its existence. It is usually associated with the name Kondratieff, a Russian economist who discovered significant long-term cycles in various price series. This Kondratieff (or long-wave) cycle is usually assigned an average length of 54 years, although the precise length varies considerably from one cycle to another. Belief in such a cycle has been greatly enhanced in recent years, in which comparisons with the 1920s and 1930s have become ever more pronounced (e.g. high unemployment, falling inflation rates, high real interest rates, falling commodity prices).

As I say, both the business cycle and any longer-wave economic cycle are inevitably of somewhat variable and uncertain length. One great advantage of the one-year seasonal cycle is that there is no doubt about its length: by definition, where such a cycle exists, it has a period of 12 months. This makes an analysis of seasonal patterns much more 'robust' and repeatable than is the case with the other cycles.

Since the seasonal effects are, in many cases, also quite pronounced, it is surprising that so little attention has generally been paid to them in the past.

I hope that this book will have gone some way to correcting that situation; also, that it will stimulate other people to undertake more detailed research into the subject.

APPENDIX I
The Mathematical Analysis of Seasonal Factors

(a)   Methods of seasonal analysis

Chapter 3 introduced you to the basic ideas behind the estimation of seasonal factors, using 12-month moving averages. This method has been in use for very many years and, simple though it is, nothing has been developed to replace it as the basic tool for seasonal analysis. Other methods have been used – and I shall briefly mention the most important alternative – but none has the simplicity and flexibility of the moving average method. Most research, therefore, has been devoted to finding ways of improving the moving average method; most of this chapter is devoted to summarizing the results of that work.

What constitutes a good method? In other words, if two different methods produce slightly different results, how do we decide which is the more accurate?

There is no such thing as a 'best' method. It's never going to be possible to allocate perfectly the monthly changes in a series of data to the various components; i.e. to the changes which are due to: (a) trend and cyclical effects; and (b) seasonal effects. Different methods may produce slightly different estimates of these effects; if so, they will also produce slightly different values for the residual, random variation which cannot be explained by trends, cycles and seasonal effects. What matters is that there is no evidence of seasonality left in those residuals. Different methods of calculating seasonal effects can each give slightly different values for those residuals, but each set of such residuals can itself be quite random.

Regression methods

Statisticians normally aim for explanatory equations which minimize the sum of the squares of these residuals. The method which explicitly does just that is regression analysis. Consider, first, a simple situation in which you suspect that a series of values consists just of seasonal effects plus random variations. You could describe such a series of values by the algebraic equation

$$Y_t = a + S_1 M_1 + S_2 M_2 + \ldots + S_{12} M_{12}$$

In this equation,

- Y_t is the value of the series at time t (i.e. in the t th month).
- M_1, M_2 etc. are called 'dummy' variables; for January, $M_1 = 1$ and all of the other Ms $= 0$; similarly, for February, $M_2 = 1$ and all of the other Ms $= 0$; and so on.

The regression analysis then calculates the values of the coefficients a, S_1, $S_2 \ldots S_{12}$ which minimize the sum of squares of the residual variations (i.e. the amounts by which the actual data for each month differ from the values predicted by the equation). The values calculated for the Ss are then the seasonal factors.

In practice, time series are likely to exhibit trends and/or cycles, as well as seasonal effects; indeed, such trends and cycles often dominate the seasonal factors. It is then necessary to introduce other terms into the equation to describe these trends and cycles. The introduction of such polynomial or trigonometric terms makes it, in my view, a rather cumbersome method. Other analysts cast more serious doubts on its value, e.g.:

No regression methods have yet been demonstrated empirically to provide sufficiently accurate estimates of the trend cycle and the seasonal.

This comment is by advocates of the X-11 method (Shiskin, Young and Musgrove). Meanwhile, other statisticians claim that regression methods are, in fact, superior to other methods. What impresses me most about the argument is that hardly anyone actually uses regression methods in practice to calculate seasonal factors. In the few examples which I have seen I have had serious doubts about the results, because of the inadequate way in which the equation has catered for all of the non-seasonal ups and downs of the time series.

There is one set of circumstances in which fairly complicated regression methods *are* preferable. That is when you want to *predict* the next few values of a time series from the earlier data – not just the seasonal components of those values, but the values themselves (including trend, cyclical *and* seasonal components). The rather complex mathematical methods involved are described in considerable detail in *Time Series Models*, by A. C. Harvey.

We are not concerned, in this book, with such questions of prediction. For our descriptive purposes, the great advantage of the moving average technique is its simplicity: there is no need to set up an equation in advance, to explain the movements in the underlying (seasonally adjusted) variations; the method automatically calculates the shape of this underlying trend-cycle, however complicated it may be.

The variation most commonly used by official statisticians is the X-11 method of the US Bureau of the Census. It is therefore the method which I should like to describe in more detail.

The X-11 method

X-11 starts by calculating the centred 12-month moving average, as described in Chapter 3. It then goes on to apply various corrections and smoothing techniques.

Deviations from the moving average are normally calculated by what is called the 'ratio-to-moving average' method (otherwise known as the 'multiplicative method'). In other words, for each month of each year, a seasonal-plus-irregular component is calculated by dividing the actual result for each month by the moving average calculated for that month. If an actual value is 20 per cent above its moving average, this would appear as a value of 120.0.

The option is available to calculate actual arithmetic deviations from the moving averages, rather than ratios; so, for instance, in analysing retail sales, the deviation could be calculated in millions of dollars rather than as a ratio.

Prior correction for 'trading days'

Part of the sophistication of X-11 lies in its ability to adjust for the different number of trading days in each month. There are two ways of doing this, which we can describe respectively as 'explicit' and 'implicit' adjustments. The 'explicit' adjustments are those defined by the user, based on his knowledge of the series being analysed. For instance, the number of recorded births in each month could be explicitly adjusted by the known number of days in each month. Similarly, for marriages, prior corrections could be specified to account for the fact that Easter may occur in either March or April.

The problem is often not just to correct each month's data for the different total number of trading days; it is often more important (e.g. with retail sales) to know the frequency of each individual day of the week: months with five Saturdays will have higher retail sales than months with four Saturdays, even if the total number of trading days is the same in both cases. That is still not the whole story: what we need to know is just *how* much more significant are Saturdays than, say, Mondays as far as retail sales are concerned. A particular feature of X-11 is an 'implicit' calculation of this effect; the program uses the data themselves to calculate the weights which should be given to each specific day of the week.

Adjustment for outliers

It is possible to request the program to reject automatically (as outliers) any data points falling outside certain limits. Typically, this might mean points for which the initial calculation assigns a random component which is more than 2.5 standard deviations from zero.

I have already explained in Chapter 3 that I am not, in principle, in favour of using this kind of option. Extreme values can arise from any one of a number of causes. For instance, an unusual spell of weather could affect very many series of data. I'm very dubious about the logic of discarding extreme results in such cases. After all, although unusual events are — by definition — infrequent occurrences, they are nevertheless just as likely to occur in the future as in the past. If we ignore the few apparently extreme months in the historical data, we are likely to produce an unrealistically precise estimate of the confidence limits of the seasonal factors; we shall then be very disappointed when we find that the data for future months keep falling outside the confidence limits which we have calculated. It's almost a general rule, in applying the results of statistical analysis, that extreme values subsequently occur much more frequently than would be expected from the analysis.

This problem can have very serious practical consequences. For instance, statistics *may* suggest that a 'melt-down' at a nuclear power station is likely to occur only once in 10,000 years; it is extremely annoying if it actually happens in our life-time!

If we are more reticent about treating apparent outliers as spurious results (to be corrected for), we shall calculate statistical coefficients which appear to be rather more imprecise and subject to wide margins of error, but that is probably what they are anyway.

Calculation of trend and cyclic effects

On various occasions in this book I have illustrated, not only the seasonal pattern, but also the long-term pattern which is left after eliminating the seasonal component. This has been done using just the straightforward centred 12-month moving average to indicate any underlying trends or cycles.

The X-11 program uses a more refined technique which further smooths this simple 12-month moving average. For each month the program calculates a weighted moving average centred on the month in question, but also giving weight to the simple moving averages on either side of it. This technique is particularly useful when the random, irregular component is high compared with the 'predictable' components (the trend/cycle and seasonal effects).

Occasionally, in Parts II and III, I used a very simple alternative to this method. You may recall that, in a few cases (e.g. exchange rates), the monthly factors which I showed were themselves 3-month moving averages. For instance, in those cases, the seasonal factor shown for January was actually the average of the factors for December, January and February.

Use of the results: description v. prediction

The simple moving average method, which I have used, calculates the average seasonal pattern for the whole of the period of the data. These average results are just what we need to *describe* the average seasonal pattern over a period of several years. On the other hand, if we want to use seasonal analysis for *predictive* purposes, we would probably want to give more weight to the more recent data. The X-11 program calculates smoothed seasonal patterns for each year: an example of this is given below. The program also calculates the *expected* seasonal pattern for the forthcoming year. This is one of the most important features of X-11, especially if the seasonal pattern is itself something that tends to vary over the years. It is a particularly important facility when you are using the analysis to seasonally correct each new month's data as they become available.

Comparison of results

In describing X-11, the Bureau of Census has presented a worked example on a set of actual data which we can use for comparison (Shiskin, Young and Musgrove). The data are for the values of US retail sales for each month from 1953 to 1964. The data are not necessarily typical, inasmuch as the seasonal factors are fairly consistent from year to year.

I'll first of all summarize some results (see table overleaf), and then discuss the implications.

It is immediately clear that the simple moving-average program produces results which are virtually identical to the average 'unadjusted' results from X-11. It is only when the X-11 program has been adjusted for extreme values, etc. (a process which I have eschewed) that differences arise — and, even then, they are very slight.

You will also see how X-11 produces separate seasonal patterns for each

**Comparison of seasonal factors calculated by the X-11
and simple moving average methods**

	J	F	M	A	M	J	J	A	S	O	N	D
X-11 individual seasonal factors (examples)												
1954	89.5	86.0	97.7	99.5	102.6	102.9	99.6	100.5	98.9	101.6	100.8	120.6
1959	90.3	85.0	96.9	99.4	103.2	103.2	99.8	100.8	97.3	101.7	101.2	121.2
1964	89.8	84.9	97.4	99.5	103.3	102.3	99.6	99.8	96.2	103.0	102.9	121.3
1953 – 64 averages												
Unadjusted	89.8	85.3	97.1	99.7	103.0	102.9	99.5	100.7	97.6	102.5	101.2	120.3
Adjusted*	89.9	85.2	97.3	99.5	103.0	102.9	99.7	100.4	97.6	102.0	101.5	121.1
Simple moving average method												
	89.9	85.4	97.1	99.7	103.0	103.0	99.6	100.7	97.6	102.6	101.2	120.4

*Adjusted for extreme values and trading days.

year. In fact, I have reproduced only three of the individual years' results — at the beginning, middle and end of the period — although results are given in the original paper for each year.

Problems attributed to moving average methods

Two main criticisms have, in the past, been levelled against moving average techniques. First, it has been suggested that the process of calculating moving averages can itself generate apparent (but spurious) cyclical patterns. Secondly, it has also been suggested that *most* methods (not just those based on moving averages) tend to over-estimate the magnitude of the seasonal factors.

I thought that it might be useful to check the first point, to see whether the method might introduce spurious seasonal effects. In order to do this, I carried out an analysis on a purely random series of numbers. I generated an imaginary 8-year series of values by selecting at random from a normal distribution with a mean of zero and a standard deviation of 100. No significant seasonal effect was generated.

Furthermore, the individual deviations from the 12-month moving averages were perfectly random and showed no evidence of serial correlation.

As to the second criticism, there may well be some truth in it. I have, myself, come across seasonally adjusted series which seem to exhibit residual seasonal patterns which are the inverse of the original pattern. In practice, these residual effects are very small; if a seasonal analysis were to be carried out on the seasonally adjusted series, no remaining *significant* seasonal pattern would be detectable.

Neither of these two possible problems is of as much concern as the question of step-changes in the data series.

Step-changes or 'shocks'

I mentioned this question briefly in Chapter 3, and would like to expand on it here.

The situation which we are considering can be illustrated by a simple, hypothetical example as follows. Consider, first, a series (e.g. a price series) which shows a sudden jump upwards in an otherwise steady pattern:

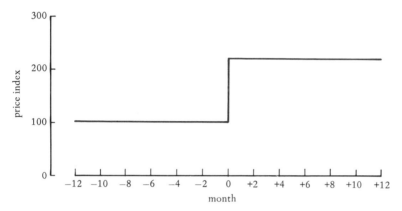

The step-change is taken to occur during what we shall regard as month '0', and other months will be counted forwards and backwards from that month. For all months up to month '0', the value which we are measuring (in this case, the price index) is 100; in month '0' it jumps to 220 and then remains at this higher level. What happens is that the moving average technique cannot react instantaneously to a step-change, and instead operates as if the change from a level of 100 to a level of 220 occurs smoothly as indicated by the dotted line in the next diagram:

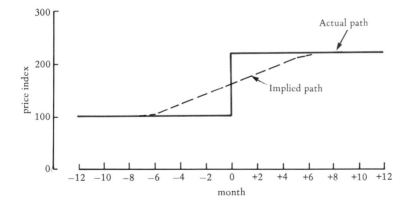

The effect of this is to induce an apparent seasonal effect which looks like this:

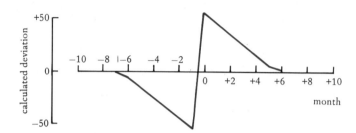

rather than an instantaneous step-change.

The sharp jump at month '0' is quite accurately reproduced, but in addition (or as a consequence), the method produces implicit seasonal factors for the other months as well. In particular, it produces seasonal factors for months which have passed into history before the step change occurs.

Cyclical changes produce similar effects, although not quite so dramatic. After a period of recession, there can be quite a sudden turnround of confidence and economic activity, at the start of a new upward movement in the economy. Because the moving average technique takes a little time to 'catch up' with such sudden changes, it induces a spurious negative seasonal effect in the months before the upturn and a positive effect in the months following the upturn (as illustrated above).

This effect is shown up very clearly if you study the output from the computer analysis. (An example of this is shown in the next chapter.)

There are two consequences of this. First, it is important to average the results over several years; any errors induced by this phenomenon will then tend to cancel each other out, and will in any case be quite small.

Secondly, this phenomenon increases the apparent size of the random, irregular component of the time series. It thus affects our estimate of the statistical significance of the seasonal effects. The measure of significance is the extent to which the seasonal variations are greater than the random effects. If these random effects are increased, then the seasonal effects would appear to be less significant than they really are. In other words, for any series of data which is characterized by strong cyclical effects (which means virtually all economic series), the true significance of the seasonal factors will actually be *greater* than suggested by the statistical analysis.

Summary

The moving-average technique has stood the test of time and no superior alternative analysis has been developed. For straightforward descriptive purposes, the simple moving average method is perfectly adequate. Where a more sophisticated analysis is required (e.g. to account for trading day variations and substantial changes in the seasonal pattern) the X-11 method offers every reasonable facility.

For the future, I'm sure that there is little to be gained by seeking further refinements. Research effort will be much more usefully spent on analysing the significance and meaning of the actual seasonal patterns which can be detected in so many economic series.

(b)   The computer program

This section describes the computer program which was developed by the Cornwall ITeC for carrying out the analyses presented in this book.

The program operates on either monthly or quarterly data, for any number of years up to 20. It could, of course, be easily adapted to consider longer time periods, although it is probably better to break down very long series into shorter components.

The main steps in the program are:

1 Calculating the moving average.
2 Calculating the deviations of individual data points from the moving average.
3 Calculating the seasonal factors — i.e. the average deviations for each month (or quarter) of the year, averaged over the lifetime of the data series.
4 Calculating the statistical significance of the seasonal factors.
5 Printing out the results in both numerical and graphical form.

The option is available to choose either an arithmetic or ratio method of calculation. In other words, the calculations can be carried out on either:

(a) the original data — in which case, the final results are in the form of arithmetic differences from the moving averages; or
(b) logarithms of the original data — in which case, the results are in the form of percentage variations from the moving average.

The logarithmic transformation is to be preferred where there is a general upward trend in the data, or in any case where the data cover a very wide range of positive values. It is analogous to the ratio option available with the X-11 program.

An advantage of the program is that it is extremely simple to use for a very large number of data series. It is most simply illustrated by showing examples of the print-out.

Arithmetic option

The example illustrated in Figure A1 overleaf is that for the CBI survey on 'output expectations'. There is no particular trend (up or down) in the data; in fact, the most pronounced feature is the strong cyclical nature of the series (see Figure 16.2). Also, the series contains both positive and negative figures. It is therefore not appropriate to choose the logarithmic option; the calculations are straightforward arithmetic differences from the moving averages.

The print-out starts with a record of the data which was fed in. This is followed by the calculated moving averages. The third block of the print-out gives the seasonal (plus random) factor calculated for each month for each year: i.e. the difference between the original data and its moving average. The heading 'standard difference', rather than just 'difference', indicates that these differences have been adjusted so that they all add up in total to zero. These standard differences for each month are then averaged over the whole time period to give the calculated seasonal factors.

The next question is whether these seasonal factors are statistically significant, or whether they could have arisen just by reason of the purely random, non-seasonal variations which occur in any series of data. The method employed in the program is to carry out an 'analysis of variance'. This compares the degree of variability *between* the monthly averages with the year-to-year variability which exists *within* a month. The latter, within-month, variation can be taken as a good measure of purely random effects. The more significant the seasonal effect, the higher will be the ratio of the 'between months' to the 'within months' variability. For the seasonal pattern to be regarded as significant, this ratio needs to exceed the appropriate figure shown in the following table:

No. of years' data	3	4	5	6	8	10
Critical ratio	2.72	2.22	2.06	1.99	1.93	1.88

There is only a 1-in-20 chance that what is actually a non-seasonal pattern of data would give such an 'F-ratio' in excess of the tabulated figure. In the example illustrated, based on 10 years' data, the calculated ratio is 2.75; this is a value which, in fact, has a less than 1-in-100 probability of being a chance occurrence.

Results using 'True' data analysis of seasonal factors
CBI Survey – Output

Original data

Year												
1975	-12.000	-11.000	-16.000	-16.000	-19.000	-13.000	-11.000	-11.000	-12.000	-1.000	10.000	2.000
1976	6.000	20.000	25.000	26.000	33.000	37.000	33.000	35.000	40.000	28.000	24.000	23.000
1977	22.000	22.000	25.000	23.000	19.000	18.000	17.000	16.000	21.000	23.000	19.000	24.000
1978	19.000	22.000	22.000	16.000	19.000	12.000	17.000	19.000	21.000	22.000	22.000	28.000
1979	10.000	19.000	25.000	24.000	27.000	20.000	4.000	1.000	2.000	4.000	3.000	-3.000
1980	-11.000	-11.000	-12.000	-14.000	-24.000	-36.000	-41.000	-43.000	-48.000	-31.000	-40.000	-36.000
1981	-16.000	-17.000	-13.000	-4.000	-1.000	-3.000	1.000	2.000	2.000	0.000	1.000	-1.000
1982	1.000	3.000	4.000	4.000	-2.000	4.000	-3.000	-8.000	-7.000	-4.000	-9.000	-11.000
1983	-5.000	8.000	16.000	22.000	18.000	19.000	17.000	19.000	20.000	16.000	24.000	27.000
1984	20.000	30.000	32.000	20.000	23.000	19.000	16.000	16.000	12.000	13.000	14.000	18.000

Moving averages

Year												
1975	0.000	0.000	0.000	0.000	0.000	0.000	-8.417	-6.375	-3.375	0.083	4.000	8.250
1976	12.167	15.917	20.000	23.375	25.167	26.625	28.167	28.917	29.000	28.875	28.167	26.792
1977	25.333	23.875	22.292	21.292	20.875	20.708	20.625	20.500	20.375	19.958	19.667	19.417
1978	19.167	19.292	19.375	19.375	19.458	19.750	19.542	19.042	19.042	19.500	20.167	20.833
1979	20.625	19.333	17.792	16.250	14.708	12.625	10.458	8.333	5.542	2.417	-1.292	-5.750
1980	-9.958	-13.667	-17.583	-21.125	-24.375	-27.542	-29.125	-29.583	-29.875	-29.500	-28.125	-25.792
1981	-22.667	-19.042	-15.083	-11.708	-8.708	-5.542	-3.375	-1.833	-0.292	0.750	1.042	0.958
1982	0.750	0.167	-0.625	-1.167	-1.750	-2.583	-3.250	-3.292	-2.583	-1.333	0.250	2.042
1983	3.833	5.792	8.042	10.000	12.208	15.167	17.792	19.750	21.333	21.917	22.042	22.250
1984	22.208	22.042	21.583	21.125	20.583	19.792	0.000	0.000	0.000	0.000	0.000	0.000

Standard differences

Year												
1975	0.000	0.000	0.000	0.000	0.000	0.000	-2.804	-4.845	-8.845	-1.304	5.780	-6.470
1976	-6.387	3.863	4.780	2.405	7.613	10.155	4.613	5.863	10.780	-1.095	-4.387	-4.012
1977	-3.554	-2.095	2.488	1.488	-2.095	-2.929	-3.845	-4.720	0.405	2.821	-0.887	4.363
1978	-0.387	2.488	2.363	-3.595	-0.679	-7.970	-2.762	-0.262	1.738	2.280	1.613	6.946
1979	-10.845	-0.554	6.988	7.530	12.071	7.155	-6.679	-7.554	-3.762	1.363	4.071	2.530
1980	-1.262	2.446	5.363	6.905	0.155	-8.679	-12.095	-13.637	-18.345	-1.720	-12.095	-10.429
1981	6.446	1.821	1.863	7.488	7.488	2.321	4.155	3.613	2.071	-0.970	-0.262	-2.179
1982	0.030	2.613	4.405	4.946	-0.470	-1.637	0.030	-4.929	-4.637	-2.887	-9.470	-13.262
1983	-9.054	1.988	7.738	11.780	5.571	3.613	-1.012	-0.970	-1.554	-6.137	1.738	4.530
1984	-2.429	7.738	10.196	-1.345	2.196	-1.012	0.000	0.000	0.000	0.000	0.000	0.000

Averages

-3.049	2.257	5.132	4.178	3.539	0.113	-2.267	-3.049	-2.461	-0.850	-1.544	-1.998

Analysis of variance

	Sum of squares	D.F.	Variance
between months	884.728	11.	80.430
within months	2813.002	96.	29.302
Total	3697.729	107.	34.558

Confidence limits based on within-months variance = 3.609

224

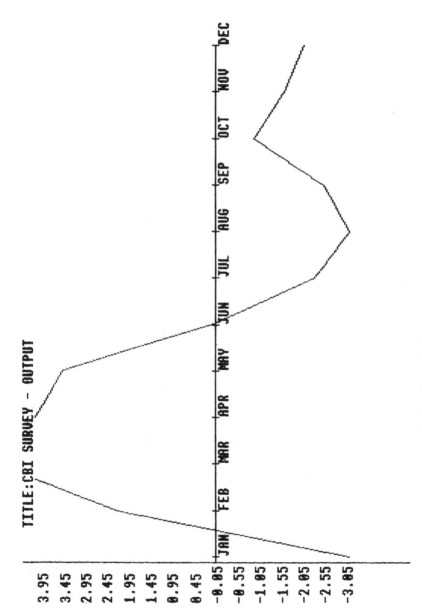

Fig. A1 Example of output: (a) arithmetic method

Results using Logarithmic values
analysis of seasonal factors
U.S. Retail 1953–64

Original data

1953	12.90	12.20	13.71	14.12	14.52	14.44	14.25	14.04	13.95	14.82	13.83	16.31
1954	12.21	11.95	13.58	14.02	14.12	14.53	14.26	13.77	14.01	14.54	14.40	17.74
1955	13.15	12.64	14.61	15.07	15.33	15.60	15.38	15.48	15.76	15.68	15.75	19.12
1956	13.73	13.55	15.53	15.94	16.11	16.58	15.26	16.19	15.58	16.13	16.49	19.38
1957	14.74	14.06	15.46	16.36	17.20	17.11	16.86	17.49	16.33	16.95	17.13	19.84
1958	15.29	13.78	15.94	16.97	17.36	16.60	16.60	17.00	17.57	17.36	17.04	21.17
1959	16.22	14.96	16.97	17.82	18.60	18.71	18.33	18.05	17.85	19.10	17.64	21.45
1960	15.80	15.83	17.63	18.97	18.55	18.92	18.07	18.15	18.16	18.65	18.38	22.15
1961	17.01	15.07	17.71	17.62	18.53	18.91	17.92	18.32	18.86	18.76	19.22	22.88
1962	18.26	16.04	19.19	19.10	20.23	20.25	19.14	19.92	19.27	20.58	20.91	24.13
1963	19.15	17.09	19.65	20.52	21.23	20.74	20.54	21.02	21.31	21.53	21.49	25.10
1964		18.76	20.50	21.19	22.51	22.24	22.14	21.78		22.60	21.72	27.72

Logarithmic values

1953	1.11059	1.08636	1.13704	1.14983	1.16197	1.15957	1.15381	1.14737	1.14457	1.17085	1.14082	1.21245
1954	1.08672	1.07737	1.14675	1.14675	1.14983	1.16227	1.15412	1.13893	1.16444	1.16256	1.15836	1.24895
1955	1.11893	1.10175	1.16465	1.18893	1.18554	1.19312	1.18355	1.18977	1.19756	1.19535	1.19728	1.28149
1956	1.13767	1.13194	1.19117	1.17811	1.20710	1.21958	1.18696	1.20925	1.19257	1.20763	1.21722	1.28735
1957	1.16850	1.14799	1.20249	1.21165	1.23553	1.23325	1.22686	1.24279	1.21405	1.22917	1.23376	1.29754
1958	1.18441	1.13925	1.18921	1.21378	1.23955	1.22011	1.22011	1.23045	1.21299	1.23955	1.23147	1.32572
1959	1.21005	1.17493	1.22968	1.25091	1.26951	1.27207	1.26316	1.25648	1.24477	1.28103	1.24650	1.33143
1960	1.19866	1.19948	1.24625	1.27807	1.26834	1.27692	1.25696	1.25888	1.25164	1.27068	1.26435	1.34537
1961	1.23070	1.17811	1.24822	1.24601	1.26788	1.27669	1.25334	1.26293	1.25912	1.27323	1.28375	1.35946
1962	1.26150	1.20520	1.28307	1.28103	1.30600	1.30643	1.28194	1.29929	1.27554	1.31345	1.32035	1.38256
1963	1.28217	1.23274	1.29336	1.31218	1.32695	1.31681	1.31260	1.32263	1.28488	1.33304	1.33224	1.39967
1964		1.27323	1.31175	1.32613	1.35238	1.34713	1.34518	1.33806	1.32858	1.35411	1.33686	1.44279

Moving averages

1953	0.0000	0.0000	0.0000	0.0000	0.0000	0.0000	1.1469	1.1456	1.1450	1.1447	1.1441	1.1437
1954	1.1438	1.1435	1.1432	1.1429	1.1433	1.1456	1.1484	1.1508	1.1531	1.1562	1.1595	1.1622
1955	1.1648	1.1681	1.1723	1.1758	1.1788	1.1818	1.1839	1.1860	1.1883	1.1890	1.1894	1.1914
1956	1.1927	1.1936	1.1942	1.1946	1.1959	1.1970	1.1985	1.2005	1.2016	1.2035	1.2060	1.2078
1957	1.2100	1.2131	1.2154	1.2172	1.2188	1.2199	1.2210	1.2213	1.2203	1.2199	1.2201	1.2198
1958	1.2189	1.2181	1.2176	1.2180	1.2183	1.2194	1.2216	1.2242	1.2273	1.2306	1.2334	1.2368
1959	1.2407	1.2436	1.2460	1.2491	1.2514	1.2523	1.2526	1.2538	1.2555	1.2573	1.2584	1.2585
1960	1.2585	1.2583	1.2587	1.2586	1.2586	1.2602	1.2602	1.2587	1.2579	1.2567	1.2553	1.2553
1961	1.2551	1.2552	1.2561	1.2561	1.2570	1.2584	1.2603	1.2627	1.2653	1.2682	1.2713	1.2741
1962	1.2765	1.2793	1.2815	1.2838	1.2870	1.2895	1.2917	1.2942	1.2958	1.2975	1.2997	1.3010
1963	1.3027	1.3049	1.3063	1.3075	1.3088	1.3100	1.3116	1.3141	1.3166	1.3179	1.3196	1.3219
1964	1.3245	1.3265	1.3290	1.3317	1.3327	1.3347	0.0000	0.0000	0.0000	0.0000	0.0000	0.0000

Standard differences

1953	0.0000	0.0000	0.0000	0.0000	0.0000	0.0000	0.0069	0.0019	-0.0004	0.0262	-0.0032	0.0688
1954	-0.0570	-0.0660	-0.0102	0.0039	0.0066	0.0057	0.0057	-0.0118	-0.0066	0.0064	-0.0010	0.0868
1955	-0.0458	-0.0663	-0.0076	0.0132	0.0068	-0.0003	-0.0003	0.0039	0.0093	0.0064	0.0079	0.0901
1956	-0.0549	-0.0616	-0.0030	-0.0164	0.0014	-0.0115	-0.0115	0.0089	-0.0090	0.0042	0.0113	0.0796
1957	-0.0415	-0.0650	-0.0128	-0.0054	0.0113	0.0060	0.0060	0.0216	-0.0062	0.0094	0.0137	0.0779
1958	0.0344	-0.0788	-0.0283	-0.0041	0.0168	0.0134	-0.0014	0.0063	-0.0143	0.0090	-0.0018	0.0890
1959	-0.0306	-0.0686	-0.0163	0.0019	0.0213	0.0008	0.0106	0.0028	-0.0106	0.0238	-0.0118	0.0730
1960	-0.0460	-0.0588	-0.0124	0.0196	0.0181	0.0106	-0.0032	0.0002	-0.0062	0.0141	0.0091	0.0901
1961	-0.0564	-0.0770	-0.0073	-0.0100	0.0095	0.0184	-0.0069	0.0002	-0.0061	0.0051	0.0125	0.0854
1962	-0.0458	-0.0740	0.0017	-0.0027	0.0010	0.0170	-0.0097	0.0052	-0.0201	0.0160	0.0208	0.0817
1963	-0.0411	-0.0721	-0.0128	0.0048	0.0191	0.0069	0.0011	0.0086	-0.0316	0.0152	0.0127	0.0779
1964	-0.0423	-0.0532	-0.0172	-0.0055	0.0197	0.0125	0.0000	0.0000	0.0000	0.0000	0.0000	0.0000

Averages

	-0.0451	-0.0674	-0.0115	-0.0001	0.0142	-0.0002	0.0043	-0.0093	0.0123	0.0064	0.0818	

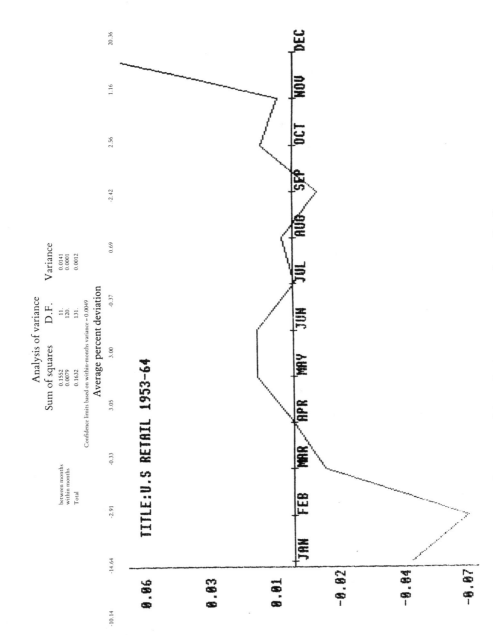

Fig. A2 Example of output: (b) ratio (or percentage) method

227

As mentioned above, the degree of 'within months' variability can be taken as a measure of random, irregular, unexplainable variation. It can therefore be used to calculate confidence limits for the individual seasonal factors. There is a 1-in-20 chance that the 'true' seasonal factor for any month or quarter could differ from its calculated value by the amount of this confidence limit, which is printed out under the analysis of variance table.

As explained in Appendix 1(a), the 'within months' variation is actually spuriously inflated if there are sharp step or cyclical changes in the data. Examples of this can be seen in Figure A1. The onset of a sharp cyclical downturn in the latter half of 1976 has caused the calculated seasonal factors to be unusually high just before the downturn and low immediately afterwards. The converse is apparent around the time of the sharp upturn at the end of 1980. This phenomenon is one reason, of course, why it is important to average the seasonal factors over several years of data. It also means that the analysis of variance is likely to *understate* the true degree of statistical significance of seasonality.

The print-out ends with a graphical representation of the average seasonal pattern which has been calculated.

Logarithmic option

The example chosen for illustration is the series of US retail sales data. (This series was used in Appendix I(a) to compare the results of the simple moving average method with the more comprehensive X-11 method.) This series, as well as having a pronounced seasonal pattern, is characterized by a fairly steady upward trend.

Compared with the arithmetic option, there are just two additional features of the print-out (Figure A2). First, the original data are additionally shown in their log-transformed form. Secondly, a further step in the calculation is needed to convert the seasonal factors (initially expressed as logarithms) into percentage variations.

It is perhaps not immediately obvious that this method (i.e. working with logarithms of the data points) should give the same results as a method which directly calculates ratios to the moving average. (For one thing, the average of a set of logarithms is not the same as the logarithm of the average.) The technical note illustrates how the two approaches do, in fact, produce the same result.

In the example illustrated in Figure A2, you can see that the very strong, consistent seasonal pattern results in a very high 'F-ratio' of over 100. It is quite beyond the bounds of probability that such a high ratio could be caused by other than a genuinely seasonal effect.

TECHNICAL NOTE

Use of a logarithmic transformation to calculate ratios-to-moving averages

The log transformation method can be shown to give the same results as a ratio-to-moving average calculation, by means of a simple numerical example. This will also show how the answers in logs are converted into percentage seasonal variations.

For simplicity, we shall consider quarterly rather than monthly data, and assume that the same pattern repeats itself exactly each year:

	Q1	Q2	Q3	Q4
Value	20	20	20	100
Moving average	40	40	40	40

The two calculations proceed as follows:

Ratio-to-moving average calculation	Q1	Q2	Q3	Q4	Logarithmic transformation	Q1	Q2	Q3	Q4
Value	20	20	20	100	Value	20	20	20	100
Moving average	40	40	40	40	Log of value	1.301	1.301	1.301	2.000
Ratio-to-moving average	0.50	0.50	0.50	2.50	Moving average	1.476	1.476	1.476	1.476
					Difference from moving average	−0.175	−0.175	−0.175	+0.524
Percentage of moving average	50	50	50	250	Antilog*	0.668	0.668	0.668	3.342
					Scale to sum to 1.00	0.50	0.50	0.50	2.50
					Percentage of moving average	50	50	50	250

(*Note that, when the difference-from-the-moving-average is negative, the seasonal factor is calculated by taking the *reciprocal* of the antilog.)

(c)   Doing it yourself

There are two ways in which you may wish to follow up your reading in a practical way. Most readers will have series of data which they would like to see analysed, so as to identify any significant seasonal effects; for instance, to indicate the best times for buying or selling shares in specific companies. In addition, as mentioned in the Preface, I hope that many readers will be stimulated to undertake some research of their own.

A wide-ranging introductory survey, of the kind which has been presented, cannot hope to go into very great detail on any one subject. Each one of the chapters in Parts II and III really needs someone to study the subject in much greater depth. There is much research waiting to be carried out, for instance to relate the seasonal pattern of one data series to those of other series, and generally to seek to explain the causes and consequences of the seasonal patterns which have been described.

The tools which you need for both of these tasks — either doing your own analysis or undertaking original research into the subject — are quite simple: the appropriate data and computer program (or bureau service).

The choice of computer program lies between the simple moving average method and the more sophisticated X-11 method outlined in Appendix I (a). A service to perform the analyses used in this book is provided by Cornwall ITeC, Daniel Road, Truro, Cornwall, TR1 2DA. Enquiries should be addressed to the Head of the Statistical Programs Unit, Mr Kevin Gleeson.

For the X-11 program, the organization to contact in the UK is CiSi-Wharton, at Ebury Gate, 23 Lower Belgrave Street, London SW1.

In addition to your own private or company data, there is of course an enormous amount of data published officially on almost anything which you can think of. Three CSO publications are especially useful: *Financial*

Statistics, Economic Trends and the *Monthly Digest of Statistics*. Other useful official publications of relevance to the businessman include the *Employment Gazette* and '*British Business*', the latter produced by the Department of Industry. For each particular industry, the appropriate Trade Association is usually a very good source of information. The larger stockbrokers are the best source of historical data for individual company share prices.

There are so many sources of information that it may be difficult to know where to start to look. Some useful summaries are:

Guide to Official Statistics, Central Statistical Office, HMSO, 1986.
Sources of Unofficial UK Statistics, D. Mort and L. Siddall, Gower, 1986.
Business Statistics Index, P. Foster, Headland Press, 1983.
Statistics Europe: Sources for Social, Economic and Market Research, CBD
      Publications, 1981.
Statistics America: Sources for Social, Economic and Market Research, CBD
      Publications, 1980.

For a wide variety of useful data series, CiSi Wharton again provide a valuable service. They are licensed by the Central Statistical Office to supply historical series of data, which are also available on-line. They supply very many more series than just those produced by the CSO and have a wide international coverage.

In all of this published information — and in your own private and/or company files — there is more than enough historical data just waiting to be analysed. I hope that this book will have stimulated many people to 'do it themselves' — not just in the UK, but in other countries as well.

Appendix II
SOURCES

(a) Sources of the data used in this book

The main source of information on the UK economy is the Central Statistical Office. Three monthly publications supply a comprehensive range of data series on almost anything you can think about; these are:

Monthly Digest of Statistics
Financial Statistics
Economic Trends

Much of the data used in this book comes from these sources. These and other sources of data used in Parts II and III are listed in this chapter. Most of the analyses were carried out using values for the years 1975 to 1984 inclusive.

Chapter 4 WEATHER
Monthly Digest.

Chapter 5 BIRTHS, MARRIAGES AND DEATHS
Births: Office of Population Censuses & Surveys (OPCS). The published monthly data were divided by the number of days in the month.
Still births, marriages, divorces, deaths: OPCS.
Road casualties: *Monthly Digest of Statistics* (published monthly figures divided by the number of days in the month).

Chapter 6 HEALTH
Prescriptions: The DHSS publish quarterly data; they kindly supplied monthly data which I converted to a per diem basis for the purpose of this analysis.

Sickness and absenteeism: Data provided privately.
Dental services and eyesight tests: *Monthly Digest of Statistics.*

Chapter 7 CRIME
Quarterly data for each full year since 1977 have been published
in the *Monthly Digest of Statistics.*

Chapter 8 EMPLOYMENT AND INCOMES
All the data are to be found in the *Monthly Digest of Statistics.*
The unemployment data refer to the level during the second
week in the month. In October 1979 there was a minor
change in the way in which the results are calculated, and I
adjusted the prior period so as to produce a continuous series
without any discontinuity.
Unfilled vacancies: data relate to the first week in the month.
Because of industrial action in 1976, which caused a break in
the series, I have started with 1977 data.
Average earnings: Some of the data are affected by large-scale
industrial disputes which will have depressed earnings for the
period of such disputes. No correction has been made for
such events.
Industrial stoppages: The data refer to the month in which the
disputes start; disputes which continue for one or more
subsequent months do *not* appear after the first month. The
figures are of the numbers of workers involved rather than the
number of disputes.

Chapter 9 RETAIL PRICES
Published in *Economic Trends.* Data for the earlier years are
published as an index based on 1970 = 100; later years on
1975 = 100. It was quite easy to 'splice together' the two series
of data.

Chapter 10 RETAIL SALES
Published in the *Monthly Digest of Statistics.* It was again
necessary to splice together different series: one from 1979
based on 1976 = 100; then a period based on 1978 = 100; and
most recently on data based on 1980 = 100. The patterns are
very consistent from year to year, so I did not go back beyond
1979.
These figures are published as weekly averages, so there was no
need to convert for the different lengths of each month.
Sales by gas showrooms and electricity showrooms are subject

to considerable later revision, although this posed no real problem. Two series did not give such a smooth transition when the base of the index was changed: these were *booksellers* and *chemists*. Particularly in the case of booksellers, there have been changes in definition (the current series includes stationers and newsagents). As a result, the data in this case are only from 1981 onwards; prior to 1981, the published figures show a much larger December peak.

Hire purchase: The data on new credit extended by retailers are given in *Financial Statistics*.

Chapter 11   CARS
Vehicle registrations: *Monthly Digest of Statistics.*
Vehicle excise duties: *Financial Statistics.*

Chapter 12   HOLIDAYS AND ENTERTAINMENT
Cinema admissions: *Monthly Digest of Statistics.*
Television: Viewing figures for 1983 and 1984 were extracted from '*ITV Facts and Figures*', issued by the Independent Television Company Association, based on data provided by the Broadcasters' Audience Research Board and AGB. I gratefully acknowledge permission to use the BARB/AGB data. Data on broadcasting receiving licences have been published from 1978 in *Financial Statistics.*
Betting & gaming duties: *Financial Statistics.*
Holidays: Statistics of the number of overseas visitors to the UK and the number of visits by UK residents were kindly supplied by the English Tourist Board, based on the International Passenger Survey.
UK airlines: *Monthly Digest of Statistics.*

Chapter 13   HOUSING AND BUILDING SOCIETIES
The statistics on building society finances are all to be found in *Financial Statistics*. The data analysed were for 1977–84.
Average prices of new dwellings are given in *Economic Trends* and include the price of land.

Chapter 14   OTHER PERSONAL SAVINGS
Published in *Financial Statistics.*

Chapter 16   BUSINESS CONFIDENCE
UK surveys: are published monthly by the Confederation of British Industry and are widely publicized in the financial

press. For historical data, I am indebted to stockbrokers de
Zoete & Bevan.

EEC surveys: are less readily accessible to the British public. In
fact, they are published in *'Eurostatistics — Data for Short-
Term Economic Analysis'* produced by the EEC. I was readily
able to acquire such data going back to 1978.

US surveys: are published monthly by the National Association
of Purchasing Management, Information Centre, PO Box
418, Oradell, NJ07649, USA.

Other countries: Data for Australia and Japan were obtained
from CiSi Wharton, who act as agents for data series
produced by the Central Statistical Office, the OECD and
various other organizations. I referred to this organization in
Appendex I(c) as it can offer a valuable short-cut to obtaining
historical series of data.

Chapter 17   STOCK MARKETS

Month-end prices for all of the major world stock markets were
kindly provided by de Zoete & Bevan.

Financial Statistics contains the detailed statistics on the various
categories of UK share prices; in this case, the data are
monthly averages rather than month-end figures.

The historical data for 1964−72 were obtained from an OECD
publication 'Principal Economic Indicators'.

The number of stock exchange transactions are given in
Financial Statistics; I have divided these figures by the
number of trading days in each month, rather than the total
number of days in the month.

Chapter 18   COMPANY START-UPS AND NEW CAPITAL

Company financing: data are published in *Financial Statistics*.
The series for rights issues goes back only to 1981.

Data on company formations is given in *'British Business'*.

Chapter 19   OUTPUT

Gross National product: *Monthly Digest of Statistics*.

Industrial output: Current data are published in the *Monthly
Digest of Statistics*. The historical information (1960−70) was
obtained from an OECD publication *'Industrial Production
— Historical Statistics'* which gives data on a wide range of
series for the period 1960−75.

Sulphur and sulphuric acid: Published in the *Monthly Digest of
Statistics*. Prior to 1981, the sulphuric acid consumption

data were shown only on a quarterly basis; otherwise these series were extracted back to 1975.

Chapter 20 COMMODITIES

The *Economist* indices, as the title implies, are published in that excellent monthly journal '*The Economist*'. I used data starting in 1976, to avoid having to correct for the change of base between 1975 and the following year. From then on, the figures are based on an index of 1975 = 100. More recent data are based on 1980 = 100. The two series can be merged reasonably easily, with one exception. As described in the text, the former 'fibres' series has now been redefined as 'non-food agriculturals'; this differs mainly by the introduction of timber as a component of the index. In this case, the recent change was too great to be able to construct one consistent series.

Monthly prices of individual commodities are published annually in the '*Commodity Year Book*'. This provides a wealth of information, not just on prices, but also on output levels, in both tabular and graphical form.

Chapter 21 OIL AND ENERGY

UK energy (and water supply): The output of this sector (which is the input to other sectors) is obtained from the *Monthly Digest of Statistics*. Because of a change in definitions, the analysis was carried out on a very short series of recent data.

Oil prices — US: *Commodity Year Book*.

Oil prices — North Sea 'Spot' oil prices are end-month estimates provided by '*Petroleum Economist*'.

Chapter 22 INTEREST RATES

UK data are to be found in *Financial Statistics*. This is also true of recent US data. The historical US data, going back to 1900, have been compiled in '*A History of Interest Rates*' by S. Homer, published in 1977. Historical UK data were taken from '*Principal Economic Indicators*' (OECD).

Another OECD publication '*Main Economic Indicators*' was the source for Japanese interest rates. For Australia, I used figures provided by the Reserve Bank of Australia in their *Statistical Bulletin*.

Chapter 24   EXCHANGE RATES

The data are most readily obtained from *Financial Statistics*, which reproduces figures given by the Bank of England. I actually based the analysis on data commencing in 1976.

Also in this chapter is the pattern for the UK terms of trade. The figures published in *Economic Trends* are subject to considerable later revision, which makes it particularly difficult to construct a smooth and consistent series. In practice I found that the impact of revisions was greatly reduced by calculating, for each month, the percentage change from the previous month; these percentage changes were used for the analysis.

Chapter 25   GOLD

The London gold price is published in *Financial Statistics*.

Chapter 26   GOVERNMENT FINANCE AND MONEY SUPPLY

These series were extracted from *Financial Statistics* and the *Monthly Digest*. In the case of all three money supply series, the factor which was analysed was the percentage change over the amount outstanding at the end of the previous month, starting with 1976. (The amount outstanding has been subject to various changes in what is and what is not included; working with percentage changes gives much more stable series of data.) Changes are recorded roughly from mid-month to mid-month.

(b) References

Barth, James R. and Bennett, James T., 'Seasonal Variation in Interest Rates', *The Review of Economics and Statistics*, vol. 57, May 1975

Britton, Andrew, 'Seasonal Patterns in the British Economy', *National Institute Economic Review*, no. 117, August 1986

Clark, T. A., 'Interest Rates Seasonals and the Federal Reserve', *Journal of Political Economy*, vol. 94, February 1986

Dewey, Edward R., *Cycles — Selected Writings*, Foundation for the Study of Cycles, Pittsburg, 1970

Diller, Stanley, *The Seasonal Variation of Interest Rates*, Occasional paper no. 108, National Bureau of Economic Research, New York, 1969

Givoly, Dan and Ovadia, Arie, 'Year-End Tax-Induced Sales and Stock Market Seasonality', *Journal of Finance*, vol. 38, no. 1, March 1983

Harvey, A. C., *Time Series Models*, Philip Allan, Oxford, 1981

Holland, T.E., *Forecasting Interest Rate Movements: Time Series Analyses and Functional Relationships*, Duke University thesis, 1963

Homer, Sidney, *A History of Interest Rates*, Rutgers University Press, New Jersey, 1977

Jevons, W. Stanley, 'Frequent Autumnal Pressure in the Money Market, and the Action of the Bank of England', *Journal of the Royal Statistical Society*, vol. 23, June 1866

Kemmerer, E. W., 'Seasonal Variations in the New York Money Markets', *American Economic Review*, vol. 1, no. 1, 1911.

Kindleberger, Charles P., *Manias, Panics and Crashes: A History of Financial Crises*, Basic Books, New York, 1980

Klein, Philip A. and Moore, Geoffrey H. *Monitoring Growth Cycles in Market Oriented Countries*, National Bureau of Economic Research, Cambridge, Mass., 1985

Macauley, Frederick K., *Some Theoretical Problems Suggested by the Movement of Interest Rates, Bond Yields and Stock Prices in the United States Since 1856*, National Bureau of Economic Research, New York, 1938

McWilliams, D. F., 'How the CBI Interprets the Industrial Trends Survey', *Twenty-five years of "ups" and "downs"*, CBI, October 1983

Marchetti, Cesare, 'Fifty Year Pulsation in Human Affairs', *Futures*, vol. 17, no. 3, June 1986

Marris, Stephen, *Deficits and the Dollar: The World at Risk*, Institute for International Economics, Washington DC, 1985

Miron, J. A., 'Financial Panics, the Seasonality of the Nominal Interest Rate, and the Founding of the Fed', *American Economic Review*, vol. 76, March 1986

Reid, D. J., 'The CBI Industrial Trends Survey — a Statistical Note', *Applied Economics*, vol. 1, no. 3, 1969

Robinson, G. N., 'Seasonality and CBI Industrial Trends Data: An Explanatory Note', *Economic Situation Report*, CBI, October 1985

Sealey, C. W. Jr., 'Changing Seasonal Movements in Interest Rates and their Implications for Interest Rate Forecasting', *Business Economics*, September 1977

Shirk, Gertrude, 'Egg Prices: 1986 Extrapolation', *Cycles*, vol. 37, no. 3, April 1986

Shirk, Gertrude, 'Soybean Prices — 1986 Extrapolation', *Cycles*, vol. 37, no. 1, Jan/Feb 1986

Shiskin, J., Young A. H. and Musgrove, J. C., *The X-11 Variant of the Census II Seasonal Adjustment Program*, Technical paper no. 15, US Bureau of the Census, 1967

Somogyi, J. de and Hall, R. J., *Retail Planning and Seasonal Forecasts for 1987 and 1988*, Staniland Hall Associates, London, 1986

Thompson, Peter and Norman, Tony, *The de Zoete Equity–Gilt Study*, de Zoete & Bevan, London, January 1986